A Taste of
OLD IRELAND

Discover Ireland's culinary secrets,
together with the legends, myths
and stories of this Emerald Isle

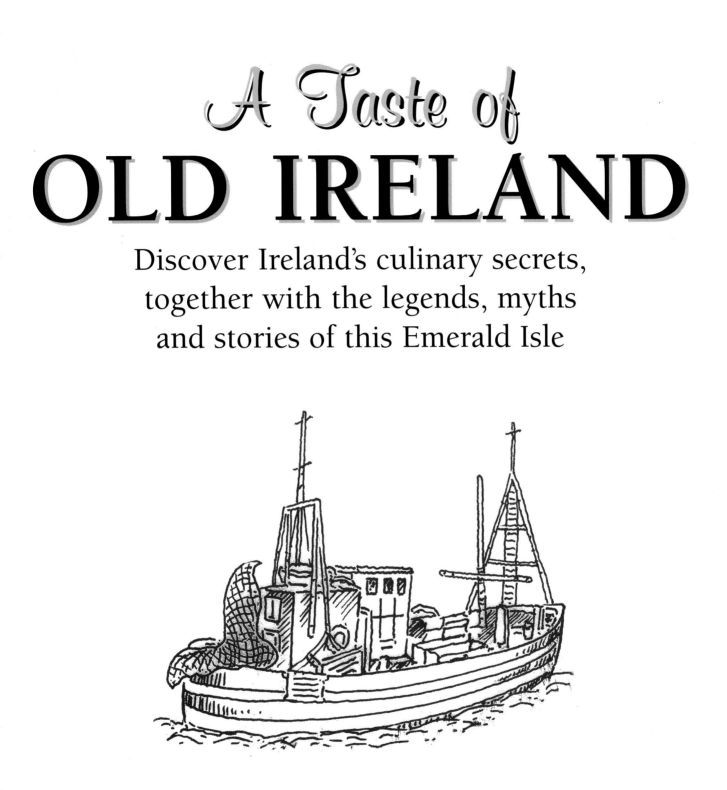

Andy Gerald Gravette

The author has made every effort to trace other copyright holders,
but if he has inadvertently overlooked any, he would be pleased to make the
necessary arrangements at the first opportunity.

Acknowledgments:
Christopher Hill Photographic; page 4-5, 13, 15, 21, 27, 28-29, 33, 36-37,
51, 57, 65, 73, 75, 77, 79, 91, 97, 99, 103, 107, 111, 115, 126-127, 129,
143, 159 and 167

First published in 2002 by Caxton Editions
20 Bloomsbury Street
London WC1B 3JH
A member of the Caxton Publishing Group

Designed and produced for Caxton Editions by
Open Door Limited, Rutland, UK.
Illustrations and photography: Open Door Limited
Setting: Jane Booth
Editing: Vanessa Morgan
Colour separation: GA Graphics, Stamford, UK

Title: A Taste of Old Ireland
ISBN 1-84067-393-1

Printed and Bound by C.T.P.S.

A Taste of
OLD IRELAND

Andy Gerald Gravette

CAXTON EDITIONS

CONTENTS

Contents

FOREWORD

A Taste of
OLD IRELAND

'So now my good people, you need never fear,

Old Ireland will prosper on this present year,

But instead of potatoes believe what I say,

We'll have a cheap loaf with a good cup of tea.'

From an Irish Broadsheet of 1847

Winnowing chaff from wheat, or drawing off curds from the whey, I've done both. But to pick out the highlights in a jewel like an emerald is a far harder task. Apart from its legendary forty shades of green, the Emerald Isle reveals a million facets whichever way you view it. Should you start with Ireland's fascinating past, wreathed in the mysterious mists of mythology and folklore, or delve into the glories of its purple mountains and verdant valleys, set against skies of indigo and cornflower blue? Is old Ireland hidden in its cloak of turbulent history, from warrior kings to starving peasantry and territorial disputes? Does old Ireland lurk in the crannies of the crofter's cottage or beneath the battlements of its lowering castles? Is the true taste of Ireland in its clear, bracing air, laced with the fragrance of heather and herbs, or in the cosy inn's snug, sharp with the tang of tobacco, and the mellow creaminess in the head of its local stout?

A taste of old Ireland is in the air, even before the visitor sets foot on its soil. The island's cultural heritage goes before it, with its literature, music, arts and science, and its legion of celebrated luminaries. To taste its cuisine is to sample the true essence of Ireland. It is in the island's food that one can really appreciate the depths of colour, aroma, texture, harmony and taste of the Emerald Isle. Separating Ireland's culinary excellence from its exotic scenery, its panoply of writers from its glorious architecture, or its Celtic background from its hospitable hosts, is like divesting love of romance. Therefore, the only way to present a true taste of old Ireland is to take a glimpse of each of its many fascinating facets and then to add a liberal collection of authentic recipes.

Advice On Cooking

As most of the recipes in this book pre-date the introduction of metric weights and measures, we have followed tradition by adhering to the original Imperial measures in which the recipes were first devised. However, should the reader prefer to use alternative culinary calculations, the following is a guide to metric and American equivalents. As with all traditional regional recipes, both ingredients and cooking methods vary from place to place throughout Ireland. Unless otherwise indicated, the recipes in this book are generally either for four people, or are part of a main dish.

Imperial Conversions To Metric

Note that the standard bottle of wine is around 26 fluid ounces, or 775ml. This is equal to 6 average wine glasses of around 129ml each.

WEIGHTS		VOLUME	
Imperial (ounces, pounds)	Metric (grams, kilograms)	Imperial (fluid ounces/pints)	Metric (millilitres, litres)
½ ounce (oz)	12 grams (g)	2 fluid ounces (fl oz)	50 millilitres (ml)
1 oz	25 g	3 fl oz	75 ml
1½ oz	40 g	4 fl oz	125 ml
2 oz	50 g	5 fl.oz (¼ pint)	150 ml
3 oz	75 g	10 fl oz (½ pint)	300 ml
4 oz	110 g	15 fl oz (¾ pint)	400 ml
5 oz	150 g	20 fl oz = I pint	600ml
6 oz	175 g	I¼ pints	700 ml
7 oz	200 g	I½ pints	900 ml
8 oz	225 g	1¾ pints	100 ml = I litre
9 oz	250 g	2 pints	I.I litres
10 oz	275 g	2¼ pints	1.3 litres
12 oz	350 g	2½ pints	1.4 litres
13 oz	375 g	2¾ pints	1.6 litres
14 oz	400 g	3 pints	1.7 litres
15 oz	425 g	3¼ pints	1.8 litres
16 oz = I pound (lb)	450 g	3½ pints	2 litres
1¼ lbs	550 g	3¾ pints	2.1 litres
1½ lbs	700 g	4 pints	2.3 litres
2 lbs	900 g	5 pints	2.8 litres
3 lbs	1.4 kilograms (kg)	6 pints	3.4 litres
4	1.8 kg	7 pints	4.0 litres
5	2.3 kg	8 pints = 1 gallon	4.5 litres

WEIGHTS AND MEASURES

As the measures and weights used in the Irish recipes in this book are traditionally Imperial in origin, these measures have been given throughout. If necessary, you can use the following tables to convert the Imperial measures into their metric or American reqivalents. In these tables, the Imperial and/or metric figures are followed by the American equivalent, where applicable. American measures use the 8-ounce cup of dry goods and liquids, and are not interchangeable with either Imperial or metric measures. The Imperial pint is 20 fluid ounces, whereas the American pint is 16 fluid ounces.

The metric and Imperial weights listed below are followed by their approximate conversions to American cup measurements, which have either been rounded up or down. Cup measures vary according to the ingredient, although a general rule for the size of an American cup is one which contains 8 liquid ounces, ½ pint, or 300 millilitres of liquid.

1 British cup equals 10 fluid ounces.
1 American cup equals 8 fluid ounces.

Although many cooks in Britain still use the British Imperial weights (Avoirdupois) and measures, metric is fast becoming the accepted method in the kitchen. Imperial does not convert easily into metric, and most recipes' figures need to be rounded either up or down, to the nearest unit of 25 grams (almost one ounce). All measurements are therefore approximate.

WEIGHTS OR MEASURES OF SPECIFIC DRY GOODS

Metric/Imperial	American
450g/1 lb of butter or margarine	2 cups (4 sticks)
100g/4 oz of grated cheese	1 cup
450g/1 lb of flour	4 cups
450g/1 lb of icing sugar	3½ cups of confectioner's sugar
450g/1 lb of granulated sugar	2 cups
450g/1 lb of butter	2 cups
225g/½ lb of castor sugar, butter	1 cup
200g/7 oz of rice, sultanas, raisins	1 cup
200g/7 oz of raw long grain rice	1 cup
170g/6 oz of brown sugar	1 cup
140g/5 oz of plain flour	1 cup
100g/4 oz of cooked long grain rice	1 cup
100g/4 oz of fresh white breadcrumbs	2 cups
100g/4 oz of butter	½ cup (1 stick)
80g/3 oz of grated cheese	1 cup
50g/2 oz of fresh white breadcrumbs	1 cup
5g/1 oz of flour, sugar	1 tablespoon

LIQUID MEASURES

Imperial	Metric	American
¼ pint	150 millilitres	⅔ cup
8 fluid ounces	225 ml	1 cup
½ pint	300 ml	1⅓ cups
1 pint	600 ml	2⅔ cups
1½ pints	900 ml	3⅔ cups
32 fluid ounces	1000 ml (1 litre)	4 cups (2 American pints)

1 British pint equals 20 fluid ounces.
1 American pint equals 16 fluid ounces.

SPOON MEASURES

The standard Imperial British teaspoon and tablespoon measurements are given in this book, and are similar to those used in the American kitchen. All spoon measurements, unless stated, are level teaspoons. Proper measuring spoons, not table cutlery should always be used. Standard spoon measures are used throughout, and all spoonfuls are level measures except where specified.

Note that the exact measurement of an Imperial tablespoon is 17.7ml, while in America it is 14.2ml. Therefore an average size is used throughout. Roughly 2 tablespoons in British measures, are equal to 3 American tablespoons.

SPOON MEASUREMENTS FROM IMPERIAL TO METRIC

1 Teaspoon = one 4 dram (5 millilitre) spoon.
I Dessertspoon = one 4.7 gram (10 millilitre) spoon.
1 Tablespoon = one 7 gram (15 millilitre) spoon.

OVEN SETTINGS

As oven settings vary so much between gas, electricity, solid fuel, fan assisted, and microwave ovens, and temperatures vary between Celsius and Fahrenheit degrees, and gas Marks, and because most of the early recipes in this book would have originally been cooked differently, basic heats are given. Where the heat of the oven is indicated in a recipe, either low heat, medium/moderate heat, or a hot oven are suggested where necessary. Oven temperatures: Both moderate and hot ovens are suggested in the recipes. A moderately hot oven should be between 160 and 180 degrees C, 325 and 350 degrees F, or gas mark 3 to 4. A hot oven should be between 220 and 230 degrees C, 400 and 450 degrees F, or gas mark 7 to 8.

INGREDIENTS

All fresh ingredients should be washed and peeled where necessary. Unless otherwise stated, all ingredients included in the recipes, like vegetables, fruit etc should be of medium size. Medium-sized eggs are used in all cases, except were stated otherwise. Pregnant women and medical patients should refer to approved guidelines before eating eggs.

Beans and pulses: With pulses, like beans, the canned variety may be used. Around half the quantity of canned pulses equals the dried, soaked and cooked equivalent. For 8 ounces (250g) of dried pulses, use a 15-ounce (432g) can of the same. Note that kidney beans contain harmful toxins and should always be fast-boiled for at least 20 minutes to destroy the toxins.

Herbs: Dried herbs can be substituted were fresh herbs are unavailable, but half the quantity indicated is sufficient.

Peppers: A warning – always prepare fresh chillis under running water if you are sensitive to their heat. Take care to avoid any contact with eyes, or other sensitive parts of the body, until you have washed your hands thoroughly.

Peanuts: A warning – a number of people can have a violent reaction even to the slightest hint of peanuts or peanut oil. In extreme cases, these reactions can be fatal.

MAP OF IRELAND

MAP OF IRELAND

ANTRIM:

The Antrim Glens host the Feis na n Gleann, celebrating the 19th-century interest in Irish culture and sport.

ARMAGH:

Named after the legendary Queen Macha, Armagh is Ireland's religious centre, selected by St Patrick in AD 445 as the country's ecclesiastical capital and seat of learning Carlow.

CORK:

County Cork is famous for its Midleton whiskey, drisheen (black pudding) and crubeens (pig's trotters).

DERRY:

Kilrea in County Derry holds an annual Fairy Thorn Festival.

DONEGAL:

In County Donegal a form of edible seaweed is found, which has the highest iron content of any food.

DUBLIN:

This is the birthplace of Guinness, with "an atmosphere which generates a drinking mood", as local writer Ulick O'Connor once remarked.

Many museums across Dublin celebrate the life and times of the country's greatest writers, and the oldest public library in the country, Marsh's Library, built in Dublin in 1701, and the Chester Beatty Library in the city, have fine collections of early botanical prints.

GALWAY:

Some of Ireland's best and most succulent small oysters come from the areas of Kilcolgan, County Galway, from Galway Bay itself, Kenmare, Clarinbridge, off the west coast, and from Strangford Lough (p.26).

KERRY:

Probably the finest veal in Ireland comes from County Kerry, where the Kerry breed of cattle is a native of south-west Ireland and is rarely seen elsewhere (p.45).

KILDARE:

Mussels are usually sold by weight, or by the measure, and the people of County Kildare swear by their mussels which come from Bannow Bay (p101).

LIMERICK:

Since the 1700s, ham in Limerick has traditionally been smoked over a fire containing juniper berries and leaves, giving it its distinctive flavour.

MAYO:

County Mayo is the location of a famous rockpool, or ocean blowhole, named the 'Poll na Seantine', or Hole of the Ancient Fire (p.111).

SLIGO:

In County Sligo there is a place called the Black Pig's grave, possibly named after a Celtic boar hunt that ended there (p.149).

INTRODUCTION

'There is no love sincerer than the love of food.'

George Bernard Shaw (1856-1950)

IRELAND is often likened to an emerald, and just as there are many ways to view an emerald – as an uncut pebble, as a many-faceted gemstone, or by selecting just one of its faces to see into its fiery heart – so *A Taste of Old Ireland* introduces snippets of early Irish life and times. Over one hundred traditional Irish recipes are included in this book, laced with a generous helping of information on their ingredients, preparation and recommended accompaniments. A little insight into Ireland's traditions and prominent sites of interest is offered, as well as potted biographies of its many great scholars. These are all woven together with tales from the island's Celtic and Christian past.

Just as it is difficult to focus on just one facet of an emerald, or concentrate on just one aspect of Ireland's life and times, so each nugget of information in this book introduces traditional recipes, mixing and matching historical myths and facts with snapshots of the beautiful countryside. More than just a book of typical local Irish recipes, the numerous anecdotes, quotations and peeps into the past serve to whet the appetite for more than a mere taste of old Ireland.

'...the turf fire was the focal point of every homestead, where travellers were made welcome, children learned the songs of old...'

'Old Ireland' is a broad term, with six millennia of history and culture to select from. Ancient sites proliferate, including one of the world's oldest Stone Age monuments at Ceide Fields, in County Mayo, and some of the best-preserved ecclesiastical edifices anywhere. Early Christian churches, soaring cathedrals, charismatic castles and fine Georgian terraces reflect the country's chequered past. But it is not just these magnificent monuments which speak of Old Ireland, it is the Irish people themselves, their mythology, folklore, traditions – and their unique cuisine. Irish hospitality is legendary and can even be dated back to the 5th century, when the Brehon Laws on etiquette and entertaining were laid down for the island's pagan kings. Back in Ireland's Celtic times, there were very particular regulations for looking after guests and for the serving of food.

These observances were handed down through generations, interrupted only by the Viking raids of the 8th, 9th, and 10th centuries, until their eventual defeat. Later, Norman invasions in the 12th century did little to endear the Irish to their unwelcomed guests. It is interesting to note that both the Vikings and the Normans – whose prime objectives had, hitherto, been rape, pillage and domination – ended up by settling down in Ireland and integrating with the indigenous Celts.

Right: the North coast of Ireland, near Ballycastle.

Just before the dawn of the millennium year of AD1000, many ancient Irish myths and fables mingled with reality as the High Kings of Ireland established their realms. The High Kings were centred around their ceremonial seat at the Hill of Tara, just north of Ireland's capital, Dublin. This citadel was a fort and palace from which the priest-kings ruled. Its ruins include a vast banqueting hall at its entrance – an eloquent testament to early Irish hospitality.

There are many references to the peculiar form of Irish cottage fireside welcome. In one, a stranger need only introduce himself by sitting by the fire and removing his brogues. Immediately, he was entitled to the laws of hospitality and afforded the status of a family member. There is an Irish saying, 'There's no hearth like your own hearth,, but the turf fire was the focal point of every homestead, where travellers were made welcome, children learned the songs of old and listened enthralled to ancient tales, handed down through the centuries. It was at the hearth that Ireland's traditional recipes were also passed down the generations. Just like colcannon and champ, the book's content chops and changes, giving the reader a blend of Irish anecdotes, together with a taste of the land. This compilation of classic and not-so-classic Irish recipes is just an introduction to real Irish fare, a taster, or sample of individual meals. In some sections, a full meal of two or three dishes might be suggested. The following 115 recipes are but recommendations, as every Irish home and kitchen produces its own version of these traditional dishes.

Chapter One

BOXTY, FARLS & BANNOCK

'The friendship of the Callans – the heat of oaten bread.'

THIS EARLY IRISH PROVERB RELATES TO THE FACT THAT OAT CAKES COME OFF THE GRIDDLE PIPING HOT, BUT – IN NO TIME AT ALL – THEY HAVE COOLED DOWN!

Old as its language, classic Irish cookery dates back to ireland's sacred sagas, folk tales and proverbs, the origins of which are steeped in the mysterious past. Under the High Kings, who had no law-making powers, there was a system of under-kings and paramount chieftains. After the death of Niall Glundubh, King of Tara, Brien, or Bru Boru became the King of Munster in AD951, with the start of the Irish dynastic wars. Boru was one of the high kings, or 'Ri ruirech', of Ireland. As one of the 'warrior kings', he was enthroned at Cashel before installing himself at the sacred Hill of Tara. During his time and down through folklore, Boru's banquets were legendary, as was his famous hospitality. However, the Irish clans were at war with invaders from Europe, the Vikings. In 997, Boru defeated the Viking occupants of Dublin but was later killed, together with his son, at the Battle of Clontarf on Good Friday, 1014. His body was taken to rest overnight in the 6th-century monastic round tower at Swords, north of Dublin. Boru's remains are interred under the Rock of Cashel in County Tipperary, the ancient seat of the warrior chieftains and the earlier, 4th-century Kings of Munster. Boru's great grandson, Muirchertach, became King of Dublin in 1069, reigning for 33 years. Today, Tara's architectural remains include the Rath of Synods, the Royal Enclosure, and the ring fort called the Royal Seat. The name O'Brien, meaning 'son of Brien', remains to this day a common name throughout the island.

A visitor to Ireland could do no better than start the day with an Irish Fry, known in the north as an Ulster Fry. Depending on the ingredients, Irish Fry is also known as a Gentleman's, or Lady's Fry, the latter with just one egg. This is a fry-up of newly baked Irish soda bread, local egg(s), farm-fresh bacon, sausages, black pudding, mushrooms, tomatoes, and the ubiquitous local potatoes.

'Learning is like bread in a besieged town: every man gets a little. But no man gets a full meal.'

Dr Samuel Johnson (1709-1784)

Right: an Irish country kitchen.

THE STORY OF IRISH BREAD

It was the Romans who brought the use of grains to Britain and thence to Ireland. They named cereals after their goddess of the harvest, Ceres, giving us the word cereal. Most cereals are ground or milled to produce a flour for baking or cooking. Although grains – developed from the seeds of wild grasses – include rice, millet, sorghum, maize, barley and oats, it is only wheat that produces a flour with raising properties. This is because of its high content of gluten, which is the sticky, nitrogenous part of the flour that absorbs water. The more gluten in the flour, the better the raising qualities of the mix. Flours such as these are called strong, or brown, flours and are used in yeast doughs.

A dough is a mixture of flour and a liquid, usually milk or water, used in the baking of cakes and breads. While strong flours are the best flours for making bread, a softer, low-gluten content flour is used in cake baking. The flour used for making cakes and biscuits is also higher in starch content than that used for making breads. This is known as soft, or plain, flour and its high starch content ensures that the flour absorbs more fat.

Wheat flour is generally accepted as white flour, which is just the starch and gluten of the grain, with the bran and wheatgerm taken out. The wheat grain, stripped of its inedible husk, is a highly nutritious food, but it is the wheatgerm which contains vitamin E, some B vitamins, plus calcium, copper, iron, magnesium, potassium and fat. The bran is high in dietary fibre, and wheat flour, which contains the complete grain, including the bran and the wheatgerm, is known as wholemeal wholewheat flour. When around 10% of the bran is removed, the flour is known as wheatmeal. Both wholemeal and wheatmeal flours are strong, or brown flours. Self-raising flour contains a raising agent and has a low gluten content, making it unsuitable for yeast doughs. Wheat grows best in temperate climates and is currently the most widely grown and used grain of all.

Eire, the ancient Celtic name for Ireland, means 'Emerald Isle', an apt description of countryside said to boast at least forty shades of the colour green. From the olives and sage greens of herbal heaths and sedgelands, to the jades and bottle greens of mountain slopes, the wild landscape is a swirl of verdant colour. When sudden rays of sun burst through indigo clouds, or the land languishes under egg-blue skies, bright patches of pasture in shades of lime and pea-green contrast starkly with the fleecy white of grazing sheep. Ireland's loughs or lakes, and numerous rivers also reflect subtle shifts of colour from sea-greens to aquamarine. With more than 30 counties, the Irish countryside varies from low, peaty boglands to towering purple mountains. Even the counties have colourful names: Waterford, Down, Clare, Kerry, Cork, Kilkenny and Tipperary all evoke images of poetic scenery. Counties Donegal, Galway, Mayo and Sligo bring to mind the rugged, wild western coast, while County Limerick has its poetical twist.

'Boxty on the griddle,

Boxty in the pan,

If you don't eat Boxty,

You'll never get a man.'

Old Irish Rhyme

TRADITIONAL BOXTY

1 pound of potatoes, coarsely grated, and dried
1 pound of potatoes, boiled and mashed
2 medium eggs
1 small onion, finely grated
2 tablespoons of flour
2 fluid ounces of milk
2 ounces of butter
½ teaspoon of salt
½ teaspoon of freshly ground black pepper

Method: *In a bowl, add the eggs to the two types of potato. Beat them together and add all other ingredients except the butter. Melt the butter in a large frying pan. Put 2 to 3 large spoonfuls of mixture into the frying pan. Fry boxtys for 3 minutes each side until golden brown and crisp. Serve immediately with bacon or apple sauce.*

With legendary amounts of water precipitating onto the Irish soil, the island is a network of rivers and fast-flowing streams. The energy produced has long been harnessed by man, in the form of water mills, a familiar feature of the Irish landscape. In early days, oats were the main cereal ground in these mills, but barley and rye were also ground to produce flour. Often the grain was ground in the home, using a hand-operated stone mill known as a 'quern'. The Irish are renowned for their baking, which has a long history, with traditional recipes being handed down through the generations. It was not long ago that baking was done in a primitive clay pot, or Dutch oven, nestled in the hot embers of an open log or peat fire.

There are other traditional methods of cooking breads, either on a griddle set over the fire, or in a heavy pan. Breads cooked on the traditional Irish griddle tend to keep longer than oven-baked breads. There are numerous Irish forms of breads, muffins, biscuits and cakes, known locally as 'kets', mostly derived from traditional home-cooking and local farmhouse recipes. It was noted in the late 17th century that the poorer people of Ireland would often substitute potatoes for bread, as they were so much cheaper. Every family seems to have their own, jealously guarded recipes for pastries, breads and cakes. Some folk even went commercial with these recipes, notably the Jacobs family of Dublin, who, in 1885, proudly produced the city's very first cream crackers.

FARLS

1 pound of flour
1 pint of buttermilk
1 teaspoon of bicarbonate of soda
1 teaspoon of maize oil
1 teaspoon of mixed salt and sugar

Method: *Sift into a bowl all ingredients except the oil and buttermilk. Pour the oil into a well in the centre. Add the buttermilk slowly, mixing into a soft dough. After this soft dough has been achieved, do not use any remaining buttermilk. Turn out the dough and knead it for around 1 minute. Roll out into a large, thin cake. Cut a deep cross in the cake, making four farls. On a moderately hot griddle, cook farls for 8 minutes each side. Do not let the surfaces burn. Slit farls in half, then serve with butter or cream, and jam.*

Dublin stands on the east coast, a pocket-sized capital city of poetical dreams, and cradle of literary aspirations. This is the birthplace of Guinness, with "an atmosphere which generates a drinking mood", as local writer Ulick O'Connor once remarked. Ale and Irish whiskey have both fuelled Ireland's literati throughout the centuries, and many of its cities' pubs and cafes provide typical Irish fare, along with coffee, ale and spirits. James Joyce (1882-1941) once observed, "A good puzzle would be to cross Dublin without passing a pub." This remarkable Dubliner was one of the city's leading writers, celebrating the people he knew in his book, *Dubliners,* and in the semi-autobiographical *Portrait of the Artist as a Young Man.* He was born at 41 Brighton Square, in the Dublin suburb of Rathgar. Aged 20, he left Ireland for Paris in 1902. Between 1903-4, Joyce returned to his Irish homeland, beginning one of his earliest works, *Chamber Music,* in 1907. Seven years later, he penned the acclaimed *Dubliners.* *Ulysses,* written in 1922, was an intimate observation of 24 hours in

the life of Dublin, seen through the eyes of anti-hero, Leopold Bloom. The character is celebrated by afficionados on 'Bloomsday', June 16th. However, when it was published, the novel received a bitter torrent of attack for its graphic sexual content. After writing his final work, *Finnegan's Wake* (published in 1939), Joyce and his family were driven back to Zurich where, in 1940, the author died.

Bewley's Cafes in Dublin have a history dating back to the early 19th century. Bewley's Oriental Cafe, one of four in the city, together with Bewley's Hotel, is an Irish institution. This impressively ornate cafe was opened in 1927 and is the Bewley showpiece. The building was once a school, attended by pupils ranging from Thomas Moore and Richard Sheridan, to the Duke of Wellington. Just around the corner from Bewley's, on Duke Street, is Davy Byrne's, made famous in James Joyce's *Ulysses.* It was here that the character Leopold Bloom washed down his Gorgonzola cheese sandwich with mustard and a glass of Burgundy. He would have enjoyed his cheese with locally-made soda bread and a glass of Irish stout or porter. Bread and ale formed the basic diet in past times, and because one of Ireland's staple foods is its bread, there are a number of different recipes. Probably the best-known and most popular is the following recipe for Classic Irish Soda Bread, one of several, as methods vary throughout the island.

CLASSIC IRISH SODA BREAD

10 ounces of plain flour
8 ounces of wholemeal flour
1 ounce of unsalted butter
1 teaspoon of baking soda
1 teaspoon of salt
1 pint of buttermilk

Method: *Heat the oven to 400 degrees F. Sift together 8 ounces of plain and 8 of wholemeal flour. Sift again, adding the soda and salt. Rub the butter thoroughly into the flour. Pour buttermilk into the centre of the mix. Stir together to form a crumbly dough. With the remaining 2 ounces of plain flour, dust the kneading board. Knead the dough until it is smooth and elastic. Form it into a disc about three fingers deep. Dust with flour, then cut an inch-deep cross in the top of the dough. Bake in the oven for 35 minutes. Remove bread from the oven and stand it on a rack to cool.*

'Airs being played pleasantly

on the harp,

Histories being read by

the wise and learned.'

Egan O'Rahilly (circa 1675-1729),
from 'On the death of O'Callaghan'.

Ireland, or Eire, often swathed in spectral mists and shrouded in ethereal clouds, evokes the romantic past around which numerous legends have been spun. Before the Kings of Tara, in Celtic times, myths and ballads were traditionally related around the fireside hearth by 'filidh', or story tellers, often accompanied by a harpist. One of these, an expert harp player – and himself woven into a timeless tale – was named Tristan. He was also a fine hunter but later turned his skills of pursuit towards a beautiful Irish maiden. His quarry was Isolde, the King of Ireland's daughter, and she had already been promised to Mark, King of Cornwall.

Just before Mark arrived in Ireland to claim his bride, a love potion was prepared to help Isolde succumb to his attentions. Mistakenly, Isolde and Tristan drank from the same love potion and fell in love. When it was discovered that Isolde and Tristan were meeting in secret, the pair were condemned to be burned alive. However, the couple escaped, fleeing the wrath of Isolde's father and King Mark.

The King of Cornwall pursued the couple across the country. Eventually, Mark discovered Isolde and Tristan asleep in each other's arms. He could have slain them there and then, but his anger waned and he forgave the lovers. As they slept, Mark placed his sword between them, to show that he had found them. He then gently placed his own ring on Isolde's finger. Upon waking, the lovers were so impressed by Mark's mercy that they returned to the royal court. Isolde was accepted back by her father and King Mark, but Tristan was banished from Ireland. Just as there are numerous versions of this tale, so there are a variety of ways to make the traditional sweet soda bread that follows.

SWEET SODA BREAD

1 pound of plain flour
1 ounce of butter
4 ounces of currants
1 teaspoon of castor sugar
1 pint of sour milk
1 teaspoon of salt
1 teaspoon of bicarbonate of soda

Method: *Sieve flour, soda and salt into a bowl, then rub in the butter. Add the currants. Make a well in the centre and pour in the milk. Mix into a dough with a fork, then turn out and knead. Turn dough smooth side up, then cut a deep cross in the top, almost dividing it into four quarters. Place in a moderate oven and bake for around 30 minutes. The soda bread is ready when a tap on the base produces a hollow sound.*

Cork, Ireland's 'second city', located in the deep south, was one described as being like Venice without the gondolas, for waterways once permeated this inland haven. Although most of the canals have been paved over, the River Lee still meanders through the city. Cork's Gaelic name is 'Corcaigh', meaning 'a watery place', and it was from here, Ireland's 'City of Tears', that close to 2.5 million people sailed for foreign lands during Ireland's great famine in the mid-19th century. The point of departure for these emigrants was Cobh, a port just south of Cork, famous for its gothic church featuring the work of Pugin.

Cork's two markets, Coal Quay, and the English Market – once out of bounds to the Irish, now attract bargain-hunting visitors and 'culchies', or countryfolk, peddling farmhouse fare. County Cork is famous for its Midleton whiskey, drisheen (black pudding) and crubeens (pig's trotters).

Nowhere in Ireland are you ever far from a mythical site or a place of miracles, and Cork is no exception. Just north of the city stands the towering keep of the famous Blarney Castle. Celebrated worldwide on account of the millions who have literally bent over backwards to kiss the famous Blarney Stone and acquire the 'gift of eloquence', Blarney is one of Ireland's oldest and most famous castles.

Some say that the Blarney stone was originally the biblical Jacob's pillow, or that it was a gift of the 'little people' inhabiting the nearby Fairy Glen. Yet others will assert that the Blarney Stone is part of the Stone of Scone, upon which many kings of old were crowned. In the mid-1500s, the Earl of Leicester was instructed by Queen Elizabeth I to take Blarney Castle from the chief of the McCarthy clan, who held it. His every effort came to nought, but, in order to appease the Queen and avoid her displeasure, Leicester sent her numerous confusing messages about his progress. These missives, both inconclusive and misleading, Queen Elizabeth dismissed as 'all Blarney!' – hence the 'gift of the gab' became known as Blarney.

Right: Soda Farls on the griddle.

WHEATEN BANNOCK

1 pound of wholemeal flour

1 tablespoon of plain flour

4 teaspoons of baking powder

1 teaspoon of baking soda

1 teaspoon of salt

3 ounces of butter

1 pint of buttermilk

1 egg, beaten

1 teaspoon of fresh sage, chopped fine

1 teaspoon of fresh thyme, chopped fine

Method: *Sift the wholemeal flour, baking powder, salt and soda together. Rub in the butter thoroughly. Make a well in the centre and pour in the buttermilk and beaten egg. Mix in the sage and thyme, then knead into a dough. Turn onto a board sprinkled with plain flour. Cover the dough in the flour, then place it in a greased baking tin. Bake for 30 minutes in a moderately hot oven. Turn heat down and bake the bannock in a low oven for 15 more minutes.*

IRISH WHOLEMEAL BREAD

1 pound of wholemeal flour

1 ounce of fresh baker's yeast

1 dessertspoon of black treacle

¼ ounce of salt

5 tablespoons of warm water

½ pint of water

Method: *Mix flour and salt in a bowl, keeping the bowl warm. Mix the treacle with the warm water separately. Break the yeast into the treacle mixture. Let the resulting mix stand in a warm place for around 10 minutes. When the yeasty mix has become frothy, add it to the flour mixture. Warm the half pint of water and stir into the mixture. Warm a greased bread tin. Mix well into a wet dough, then place it in the tin. Cover with a warm cloth and leave in a warm place for 30 minutes. Remove cloth when the loaf has increased in size by around a half. Bake in a medium oven for around 35 minutes. When cooked and brown, the loaf should sound hollow when tapped. Cool on a wire rack.*

BOXTY, FARLS & BANNOCK

There is an old Irish saying, 'He who takes the longest to eat will live the longest' and, during the years of famine in the 1840s, many such ditties were penned on the plight of the Irish and the pleas for food made by the impoverished peasantry. As the potato crops rotted in the ground, Ireland vainly sought sustenance from abroad. Sadly, the much-needed provisions arrived too late for the many thousands who had already starved to death – and for the thousands who had left for America in search of food and work. It was during the famine that some wit wrote the lines in the box below.

Barm brack is a rich and spicy cake, made with yeast and a number of foreign ingredients unheard of in Ireland until the late 19th century. Its Irish name is 'bairm breac', which means 'speckled cake'. It was traditionally baked at Hallowe'en, when a gold ring was concealed in the cake. Whoever found the ring, according to local superstition, was supposed to get married within the year.

> '*Do not be down-hearted,*
>
> *but cheer up once more,*
>
> *The provision is coming from*
>
> *each foreign shore,*
>
> *Good beer, flour and butter,*
>
> *rich sugar and tea,*
>
> *From Russia and Prussia and*
>
> *Amerikay.*'

BARM BRACK

4 tablespoons of sugar
2 tablespoons of castor sugar
1 pint of milk
1 ounce of yeast
1 pound of flour
2 eggs, lightly beaten
2 ounces of butter
1 pound of sultanas
6 ounces of currants
2 ounces of candied peel
1 teaspoon of allspice
½ teaspoon of salt
1 tablespoon of caraway seeds

Method: *Warm the milk, then dissolve 1 teaspoon of sugar, then the yeast in it. Leave in a warm place for 20 minutes. In a bowl, mix the flour with the allspice, caraway seeds and salt. Rub the butter into the flour. When the yeasty milk starts to froth, pour it into the bowl. Beat in the eggs, then knead the mixture into a dough, folding in the fruit as you knead. Place dough in a greased bowl, cover it with a cloth, then leave it in a warm place for 1 hour. When the dough has risen, put it on a floured surface and divide it in two. Place in two greased bread tins, then bake in a hot oven for 1 hour. Make a glaze with the castor sugar and a little boiling water. Brush the warm, cooked loaves with the glaze, then return them to the oven for another 3 minutes to fix the glaze.*

There were once many corn-grinding mills in Ireland, mostly run by water. A number of these are still in place, like the 19th-century example at Annalong, in the Mourne mountains, where there were once 20 working mill wheels in the 17th and 18th centuries. Three sets of mill wheels are still driven by a tributary of the River Clare, near Tuam, in County Galway. They were constructed in the 17th century and now serve as the focal point of a corn-milling museum. Where running water was not available, there were also a number of windmills built, but few have survived.

Probably one of the best-preserved mills is that of Ballycopeland, just south of Bangor, in County Down. Built around the 1780s, when the Ards peninsula was a great grain-growing region, it was a working mill until 1915, and has been reconstructed as a working mill today. The mill complex includes the miller's house, the dust-house, and the kiln where the grain dried before milling. Blennerville Windmill, near Tralee, was built in around 1800 and worked until 1880. The five-storey mill has now been renovated and contains displays of mill operation. This is by no means the tallest existing windmill in the country, as the ruins of the mill near Dundalk stand seven storeys high. Tacumshane Windmill was built, near Wexford, in 1846 and has also been restored. There is yet another old windmill attached to the Guinness Museum in Dublin. It is known as Saint Patrick's Tower.

BREAD SAUCE

1 onion, quartered
2 ounces of fresh, white breadcrumbs
½ pint of milk
1 ounce of butter
1 bay leaf
1 tablespoon of cream
½ teaspoon of salt and freshly ground black pepper, mixed

Method: *Bring the milk, onion and bay leaf almost to the boil. Cover and set aside for 30 minutes. Strain the cooled milk into a pan. Add the breadcrumbs and stir well. Add the butter, salt and pepper, then stir in the cream. Serve warm.*

Chapter Two

BUTTER, CHEESE & CREAM

'Butter with butter is no condiment at all.'

Old Irish saying

LITERATURE'S OLDEST VERNACULAR STYLE IN EUROPE IS IN THE IRISH LANGUAGE,
DATING BACK TO AD500, AND IT WAS OFTEN PENNED BY THE COUNTRY'S EARLY MONKS.

Some Irish monks mingled folklore and legend in their early writings. The island's legends pre-date Christianity, often mingling figures from pagan history with those of mythology. Many Irish legends relate to cattle, the value of which was once measured in numbers of slaves. 'The Cattle Raid of Cooley', or 'Tain Bo Cuailnge', is one of a number of tales in the ancient 'Ulster Cycle' collection. It relates how Queen Medb of Connacht one night compares her possessions with those of her husband, Aillil. Medb finds out that Aillil's herd of cattle is just one bull stronger in number than hers, which drives her into a jealous frenzy.

At this time, the people of Connacht and Ulster were regularly raiding each other's territories and rustling their cattle. It was widely known that in Ulster there dwelt a famous bull, called the Donn of Cooley. Medb vowed to add it to her herd to redress the balance. The word 'Donn', or 'Don' – these days more commonly associated with the Mafia – was the Irish name once used for the head of a local clan.

A curse, or 'geis', had stricken all of Ulster's warriors when Medb invaded. However, Ulster's King Conchobhar had a nephew, the 17-year-old Cu Chulainn, who was not affected by the curse. The wily Queen Medb enticed the youth to fight in single combat with each of her champion warriors, which he did over a period of three months. Although Cu Chulainn emerged victorious, Medb invaded Ulster anyway and her soldiers carried off the Donn of Cooley to Connacht. When the Ulster warriors recovered from the curse, they went in search of the famous bull, which, in the meantime, had killed one of Aillil's bulls, equalizing the herds of the two Connacht rulers. But, as the Ulstermen returned to their homeland with the Donn in tow, the mighty beast's heart burst and it, too, died.

In both rural Connacht and Ulster, there are still rumours of those underworld creatures, the 'butter fairies', who steal the cream from the top of the milk. However, any cattle rustling which still goes on between the two regions is doubtfully put down to the island's 'little people'!

Soldiers of buttered Irish toast go perfectly with the local oysters. Charles Dickens once wrote, 'secret, and self-contained, and solitary as an oyster', at a time when oysters were the fare of the Victorian poor. Some of Ireland's best and most succulent small oysters come from the areas of Kilcolgan, County Galway, from Galway Bay itself, Kenmare, Clarinbridge, off the west coast, and from Strangford Lough. Although it is traditional to eat Irish oysters raw, with a drop of lemon juice and thickly sliced soda bread, all washed down with a favourite Irish stout, they can also be grilled, steamed, or sauteed, as in the following dish, which classically combines toast and lemon with the oysters.

Saint Patrick's Day, 17th March, falls conveniently in the middle of the local oyster season, when, in some shops, you can buy fresh or smoked oysters, or, alternatively, smoked oysters in tins. Oysters are commonly sold fresh in quantities, or divisions of a dozen. Generally, between 6 and 8 oysters are served per person. Reputedly, Casanova would consume 50 oysters every morning! Oysters contain vitamins, salt, calcium, iron and phosphorus, and have a high iodine content. Fresh oysters should be kept with the flat shell on top, as the deeper shell retains the liquor. Butter oysters go well with traditional wholemeal bread and might well be followed by a typical Irish dessert, such as buttermilk pudding.

BUTTER OYSTERS

Ingredients per person:
6-8 oysters
1 slice of hot, buttered toast
2 tablespoons of butter
2 lemon wedges

Method: *Open the oysters into a sieve over a bowl, conserving the liquor. Pick out any grit or shell from the oysters. Heat half the butter to foaming, then toss the oysters into the pan. After 1 minute, or just under, the oysters will be sufficiently heated through. Place the oysters on the toast. Add the rest of the butter and the liquor to the pan, then bring to the boil. Pour gently over the oysters. Serve with the lemon wedges.*

Cream is the part of milk that contains the fat. Single cream consists of 18% butterfat, while double cream contains 48% butterfat. The method of preparing clotted cream probably came to Ireland from Cornwall. It is made by standing milk for 12 hours, then gently heating it, causing the cream to form in crusty layers. The clotted cream is then skimmed off. There are two main types of butter, the first being made from fresh cream and known as sweet cream butter, the second being lactic butter made from ripened cream, to which bacterial agents have been added to improve the flavour. Both butters contain around 80% milk fat, almost 16% water, 2.5% salt, which brings out the flavour, and around 2% milk protein.

Right: oysters are commonly sold fresh in quantities, or divisions of a dozen.

The cream from around 18 pints of milk goes into making just one pound of butter, and around a third of the world's milk is made into butter. In olden times, butter was packed into wooden churns and stored in peat bogs, where it would keep well for a length of time. 'Bog butter', as it was known, has been discovered in bogs after hundreds of years, during which time it had turned into a form of cream cheese. Ireland is the fourteenth largest producer of butter in the world. With a high energy content, butter contains vitamin D and calcium, and is particularly rich in calories and vitamin A. Buttermilk is used extensively in traditional Irish cooking, often mixed with a little bicarbonate of soda as a raising agent. Buttermilk, the liquid left after churning the cream, consists of 90% water, 5% milk sugar and 3% milk protein. Its lactic acid and mineral content give buttermilk its sour flavour. The Irish have a Gaelic word, 'sniugadh', which refers to the last, and richest part of an animal's milk.

> 'There's nothing like a dairy
> if folks want a bit of worrit
> to make the days pass.'
>
> George Eliot (Mary Anne Evans), in 'Silas Marner' (1819-1880)

BUTTERMILK PUDDING

5 ounces of castor sugar
½ pint of double cream
1 pint of buttermilk
1 teaspoon of powdered gelatine
1 vanilla pod

Method: *In a cup, dissolve gelatine in 2 tablespoons of boiling water. Cut the vanilla pod in half. Place it in a pan with the sugar and half of the cream. Heat but do not boil. Remove pan from heat and stir in the gelatine, blending well. Remove the vanilla pod, then whisk the buttermilk into the hot cream. Whip the remaining cream until stiff, then fold it into the hot mixture. Pour into a bowl and chill well.*

Cheese is one of man's oldest foods and probably existed 11,000 years ago. Originally a method of preserving milk, cheese is made by curdling milk with rennet. The separated results are the solid curds and the liquid whey. The curds are drawn off and either pressed or moulded, then salted, drained, dried, cured and aged. The ripening is achieved by various methods, each producing a different variety of cheese. Cheese is rich in protein, fat, minerals and vitamin A. There are around 170 different Irish cheeses, varying considerably in texture and strength, from the semi-soft Derrynaflan cheese to the hard, unpasteurized Gigginstown cheese. Dunlop, initially an Irish cheese, was introduced into Scotland by a refugee from the religious persecution of the 17th century. It is similar to a Cheddar cheese, but with a moist, fine texture. Not only does a cheese's flavour depend on the milk used – cow's, sheep's, or goat's – but also on the pasture upon which the animal grazes. There is a Gaelic word, 'glasghaibhlinn', meaning 'very green grass, watered by a stream'. Animals feeding on this grass are thought to produce the very best milk.

Below: the dairy produce of the Irish countryside is famous the world over.

Today, Ireland is renowned for its dairy produce, especially its excellent butter, cream, and wide variety of cheeses. However, the art of making cheese, an important ingredient in the Irish diet since the early Christian times, went into a decline towards the end of the 1600s. By the mid-19th century, around the time of the Great Potato Famine of 1845, cheese-making in Ireland had almost died out. Over the past few decades, the revival in local cheese-making has produced a wonderful selection of extraordinary cheeses. Almost any hard Irish cheese can be used in the following dish, which serves four people. The great Dubliner, Jonathan Swift, once proclaimed, "Bachelor's fare: bread and cheese, and kisses."

IRISH RAREBIT

8 ounces of hard Irish cheese, grated
1 dessertspoon of cornflour
1 teaspoon of dry mustard powder
1 dessertspoon of white vinegar
2 eggs
½ pint of milk
Pinch each of salt and pepper
Dash of Tabasco sauce
1 teaspoon of paprika
4 slices of Irish wholemeal bread

Method: *Mix all the ingredients, except the paprika, in a pan. Cook slowly, stirring constantly, over a gentle heat. When the mixture is combined and hot, take it off the heat. Spread mixture on the bread slices. Grill under a hot grill until golden brown. Sprinkle a little paprika on each slice and serve straight away.*

Ireland has a wealth of historic stately houses and impressive castles, many of which are open to the public. A great number of its early castles now lie in ruins, but the oldest inhabited, Kilkea Castle in County Limerick, and Desmond Castle in County Adare, date from the 13th century. In nearby County Munster, Kanturk has a 17th-century fort, and Munster's Castle Ballynacarriga was built in the 1400s. In the same county, is the 16th-century White Castle. Dromoland Castle, a baronial home in County Clare, dates from the 1500s and is now an hotel. Near Limerick, also in Clare, is the 15th-century Bunratty Castle, while Ross Castle is in adjacent County Kerry.

One early monument is the Mussenden Temple, near Castlerock, in County Londonderry. It is listed among the 100 most endangered architectural sites in the world. There are numerous more recent castles and stately homes which have been converted to take guests. These were built by the gentry of the 1800s. Faithlegg House, in County Waterford, is a good example, as is the 19th-century Ashford Castle in Cong, County Mayo. Cong is famous for being the setting of director John Ford's 1952 blockbuster film, *The Quiet Man*. It starred Maureen O'Hara, and John Wayne – who portrays the Irish prize fighter, Sean Thornton, returning to Ireland in the 1920s. The Quiet Man Festival is held every July in this western town.

TIPSY DUBLIN RAREBIT

4 ounces of hard Irish cheese, grated fine
1 teaspoon of mustard powder
1 ounce of butter
2 tablespoons of stout
1 teaspoon of cayenne pepper
4 slices of thick brown bread

Method: *Over a low heat, melt the butter in a pan. Slowly add and melt the cheese into the butter. In a cup, mix the mustard with a little of the stout. Pour the mustard stout mix into the rest of the stout and stir. Mix this into the cheese and butter in the pan. Toast the bread on both sides. With a fork, press the centre of one side of each toast slice down, compressing it, while leaving the crust raised, to form a flat 'well'. Carefully pour the stout and cheese mix into each of the toast wells. Brown under the grill and serve immediately, sprinkled with cayenne pepper.*

Sorrel (Rumus acteosa) or Garden Sorrel, symbolizes affection, and is different from Wood Sorrel, which is used in herbal medicine. Both the leaves and stem of this perennial herb are used in fish, pea, or chicken recipes, and it is particularly good with egg dishes. Sorrel soup is a traditional favourite in Ireland's country cuisine. Sorrel contains oxalic acid, a substance which is said to be beneficial for the blood. It is also found in green bananas, rhubarb and spinach. Even the 17th-century herbalist, Culpeper, noted that this herb could "cool inflammation and heat of the blood."

SORREL SOUFFLE

1 pound of fresh sorrel, cleaned and chopped
2 ounces of butter
2 eggs, separated, and yolks beaten
4 tablespoons of hard cheese, grated
3 tablespoons of white breadcrumbs
3 tablespoons of milk
½ teaspoon of salt and white pepper, mixed

Method: *Cook the sorrel in the butter for 3 minutes. Stir in the beaten egg yolks. Soak the breadcrumbs in the milk for 20 minutes, then add to the mixture. Fill the base of a greased baking dish with the cheese. Beat the egg whites with salt and pepper until stiff. Mix the egg whites into the sorrel mixture. Pour the mixture into a baking dish and bake in a moderate oven for around 20 minutes. When the top has risen and browned slightly, remove dish from the oven. Serve as a vegetable with fish or chicken.*

The country way of making a type of Irish cream cheese was to put thick, sour cream into a cloth bag. It was then hung from the roof of the cottage, allowing the thin, watery liquid to drain out. The cheese was then placed in a hooped, wooden sieve and pressed down tightly. Traditionally, potatoes were boiled in an iron pot, over a turf fire, then strained through a wicker basket before serving. In the 17th century, the poorer folk of Ireland were reduced to a diet consisting entirely of potatoes, although they might occasionally have been served with a little sour milk. Milk was also used to colour their only available drink, water.

CHEESE & POTATO CAKES

1½ ounces of hard Irish cheese, grated
1 pound of potatoes, cooked
2 egg yolks
1 egg, beaten
2 tablespoons of double cream
2 tablespoons of flour
Pinch of dried basil
3 tablespoons of white breadcrumbs
1 teaspoon of salt and black pepper, mixed
Pinch of cayenne pepper

Method: *Press the potatoes through a sieve and keep hot. Beat the egg yolks and add them to the cream. Mix the yolks and cream into the potatoes. Stir in the cheese, then add basil and cayenne. Season with the salt and pepper. Stir the mixture thoroughly and form it into small cakes. Coat the cakes with flour and dip them in the beaten egg. Coat the cakes with breadcrumbs and fry in shallow fat. Serve when both sides of the cakes are golden brown.*

One of the first Irish blue cheeses to be made in country farmhouses was Cashel Blue, a cow's milk cheese from Tipperary, which has been compared to Gorgonzola in taste. Likened to Gouda, the Coolea cheese has an orange rind and is made from cow's milk in County Cork. It is ideal for recipes where grated hard Irish cheese is called for.

Also from Cork comes Ardrahan, a cheese also likened to the Dutch cheeses. Muleens, a product of West Cork, is a soft, spicy and creamy cheese, with the texture of Camembert. The rind of this cheese is washed in salt water as it matures. A similar cheese, made in Thurles, County Tipperary, is Cooleeny. With its white mould rind and gooey inside, it is reminiscent of Camembert.

Gubbeen, a musky-flavoured Irish cheese, is made with vegetarian rennet and unpasteurized cow's milk in Skull, County Cork. Unpasteurized cow's milk and vegetarian rennet is also used in Durrus cheese, a soft variety with a dark, pink rind. In any recipe calling for Parmesan cheese, this hard Italian cheese cannot be better substituted than with the dry and crumbly Gabriel cheese. The many varieties of Irish cheese also include those made with sheep's or goat's milk. One well-known goat's milk cheese is Inagh, from Shannon.

CHEESE AND CHIVE SOUFFLE

8 ounces of cottage cheese
4 eggs, separated
1 ounce of butter
2 tablespoons of chives, chopped fine
1 tablespoon of fresh parsley, chopped fine
½ teaspoon of salt and white pepper, mixed
Dash of Tabasco sauce

Method: *Beat the egg yolks with the salt, pepper and Tabasco sauce. Whisk in the cottage cheese a little at a time. Stiffen the egg whites with a whisk, then fold gently into the yolk mix. Add the chives and parsley. Butter a small baking dish and heat on stove until hot. Pour in the mixture and turn the heat down very low. Leave on the heat for about 3 minutes. Now place in a hot oven for about 10 minutes. When the souffle has risen high and has turned brown, serve straight away.*

Hurling is traditionally Ireland's national sport and it vies with the Basque game of jai-alai, or Spanish pelote as the world's fastest sport. The game is played by striking a ball, or 'sliotar', with a curved stick. There is a famous local tale which relates the story of a master hurling champion. The reigning

sportsman of a region sought the love of a beautiful young woman. His rival in love was a great horseman. The girl could not make up her mind between them, so she decided to set the two a challenge. Whichever of the suitors could send a love letter from one end of the island to the other, in the fastest time, would win her hand in marriage.

The equestrian arranged for his friends to stage a relay of steeds across the country, while the hurler did likewise with a team of hurling experts. The former had his letter handed from rider to rider, while the latter sewed his letter into his sliotar. Just as one love letter was passed on between the relay of horsemen, and the other was hit from hurler to hurler, so the tale has been passed down through generations of horse-racing aficionados and hurling fans. In true Irish tradition, the winner of the contest varies, depending on the sporting preferences of whoever tells the tale!

CHEESE CUSTARD

1 cupful of milk
4 ounces of grated cheese
2 eggs
Pinch of salt and pepper

Method: *Heat the milk and cheese in a pan, stirring until the cheese is dissolved. Beat the eggs well, then stir them into the mixture. Stir in the pepper and salt. Pour into a baking dish. Brown in a moderate oven for 15 minutes. Serve immediately, while hot.*

Above: Cheese and Potato Cakes.

Chapter Three

SOUPS, STEWS & CODDLES

After several generations of neglect, many Irish folk tales have been recently resurrected, and have formed the basis of several modern stories and films.

IRISH LEGENDS ARE SAID TO HAVE BEEN HANDED DOWN THROUGH THE CENTURIES OVER A PERIOD OF AT LEAST FOUR MILLENNIA.

A member of the onion family, leeks (Allium ampeloprasum) were probably brought to Britain by the Romans, who called them 'porri', and they later arrived in Ireland. For several centuries, before the introduction of potatoes, many Irish people lived on a diet of leeks, oatmeal and milk.

One of Alexander the Great's feasts at Giza, in Egypt, consisted of 'radishes, onions and leeks,' and the 4th-century Greek historian, Herodotus, recorded that the diet of the slaves who built the Great Pyramids included leeks.

This soup is characteristic of the many local dishes which do not contain meat. Leeks should be prepared by cutting off the green tops, a hand's width above the white part, and slicing off the root. The leeks should then be thoroughly washed in order to remove any dirt that lies between the layered leaves. The coarse, outer leaves should be removed. The smaller type of leeks tend to be the most tender, and are used as a vegetable, while the larger leeks are best in soups and stews. The following recipe caters for two people.

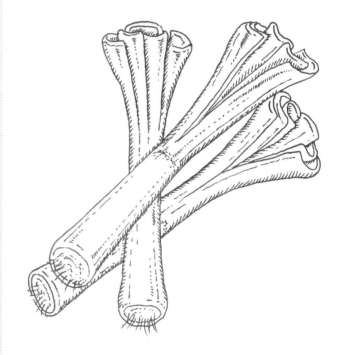

Right: before the introduction of potatoes, many Irish people lived on a diet of leeks, oatmeal and milk.

LEEK & OATMEAL BROTH

3 large leeks, coarsely chopped
2 tablespoons of oatmeal
1 pint of milk
1 ounce of butter
1 tablespoon of fresh parsley, chopped
1 teaspoon of salt
½ teaspoon of white pepper

Method: *Boil the butter in the milk over a moderate heat. After the butter has melted, stir in the oatmeal. Cook for 1 minute, stirring, then add the leeks, salt and pepper. Cover the pan and simmer on a low heat for around 40 minutes. Add parsley and bring soup to the boil. Cook for a further 3 minutes, then serve.*

Druid deities in Ireland had their own feast days, pagan Celtic festivals which have survived the invasions of Vikings, Romans, the Christian bishops and the English. Lug marks the beginning of winter, and the Romans associated the deity Lug with their god, Mercury. At this time, a celebration known as Samain, the festival of the dead, took place. In this observance, it is interesting to note the similarity between the name, Samain, and that of Baron Samadei, the voodoo god of death. In Irish lore, Lug, or 'little body', became Lug chorpan. Through the centuries it became Luparchan, evolving finally into the word Leprechaun.

'The pleasures of the table are of all times and all ages, of every country and of every day.'

Brillat-Savarin (1755-1826)

Right: Leek and Oatmeal Broth.

Christian bishops tried, unsuccessfully, to disguise pagan rituals such as Lugnasad, where the end of summer is celebrated by communities collecting the last berries of autumn, and Imbolc, which became Saint Brigit's Day, when farmers had the sheep and cattle blessed, and nailed up fertility symbols in their byres, or barns. Brigit of Kildare was originally an ancient Celtic deity, controlling fertility, poetry, music, healing and learning. Her followers gave us the word 'brigand'. Brigit was the foremost of Celtic goddesses, once a bondswoman but elevated to the highest position, with a feast marking the first lactation of ewes. Yet another pagan festival to fall foul of Roman rule was that of Beltaine, which marked the beginning of summer, traditionally celebrated on May Day.

As in so many early cultures, the original, ancient sacred places were taken over by newcomers. Wherever the Christians of old travelled, from the old Roman Empire to that of the Aztecs of Central America, they always built their churches and monasteries over, or near, the sites of pagan altars and revered locations. In Ireland it was no different, and Saint Patrick built his church on the site of Ard Macha, a twin to the holy, pagan hill of Emhain Macha.

In a challenge to the sacred hill of Tara, seat of Irish kings, chieftains and deities, Secundinus constructed his church of Dunshaughlin, directly facing Ireland's most holy site. Bishop Sacellus founded his holy citadel on the slopes of the sacred mount of Cruachain, while Mel built Ardagh church to face Bri Leith, an ancient ceremonial Celtic site. Thus it was inevitable that the Irish pagan culture would eventually integrate with that of the Christian migrants. Several of these challenges are documented by the 7th-century writings of Cogitosus. In his book *Life*, the author not only describes such everyday events as the making of butter and other traditionally Irish farming occupations, he also includes detailed reports of many miracles.

Nettles (Urtica dioica) have long been used as a vegetable in Ireland, where they are washed, cooked for 10 minutes in the water which is left on the leaves, then chopped roughly with salt and pepper and served with a knob of butter. Rich in iron, they have a slightly bitter taste. Just the tips of very young nettles should be picked, as these are the tenderest and most full of flavour. As a medicinal preparation, nettle tea is used to treat arthritis, and as a blood purifier. Oddly enough, considering its stinging qualities, the nettle is also used in the treatment of skin disorders. As early as the 6th century, Irish monks created nettle soup, when it was made solely with milk.

TRADITIONAL NETTLE SOUP

1 pound of nettle tips, washed
1 onion, chopped fine
2 potatoes, finely chopped
1 ounce of butter
6 tablespoons of double cream
1½ cups of stock
1 cup of milk
1 teaspoon of salt
½ teaspoon of black pepper

Method: *Cook the onions and potatoes in the butter for 7 minutes, stirring. Add nettles and cook, stirring for 3 minutes. Stir in the stock, milk, salt and pepper. Boil, cover pan, then simmer for 15 minutes. When the potatoes are tender, reduce soup to a puree in a blender. Return soup to the pan and bring it slowly to the boil over a moderate heat. Serve hot in bowls with a swirl of cream spooned on top.*

The foot-high chervil plant (Anthriscus cerefolium), has fern-like leaves, tasting slightly of anise. These are used in many culinary preparations, and to season omelettes, cheese and egg dishes, stews, and soups such as the one that follows here. The leaves are also used decoratively, in the same way as parsley, but chervil has a more aromatic, aniseed-like flavour. In country remedies, the chervil leaves are used medicinally to reduce fevers, and as a mild diuretic. Most potatoes can be used in the following recipe, but floury ones, like the Maris Piper, are considered among the best.

POTATO & CHERVIL SOUP

1 pound of potatoes, diced
2 large onions, chopped
6 ounces of fresh chervil
3 ounces of butter
1 bouquet garni
2 ounces of cream, whipped
3 pints of stock
½ teaspoon of salt and white pepper, mixed

Method: *In a large pan, fry the onions in the butter for 6 minutes. Add the stock, potatoes and bouquet garni, then bring to the boil. Chop the stalks from the chervil and add the stalks to the pan. Simmer for 20 minutes. Remove from the heat and allow to cool. Chop the chervil leaves finely, keeping aside a teaspoonful. Remove the bouquet garni and add the chervil leaves to the pan. Add the salt and pepper, then heat the soup to simmering point. Serve hot with a swirl of cream and a sprinkle of chervil leaves.*

After several generations of neglect, many Irish folk tales have been recently resurrected, and have formed the basis of several modern stories and films. Irish legends are said to have been handed down through the centuries over a period of at least four millennia. Some of the oldest Irish tales embrace both mythological characters and factual accounts. One of the earliest legends is documented in the *Book of Invasions*, or *Leabbar Gabbala Eireann*. It tells how the Milesians – the original Celts or Gaels – led by a mythical Spanish king named Miledh, invaded Ireland in 1500BC. This was 4,500 years after the first Mesolithic arrivals. In some tales, this leader is said to have been Nemed, a Greek Scythian. After becoming lost at sea, while searching for an elusive tower of gold that had mysteriously sprung from the waves, Nemed finally arrived on Irish soil.

The Milesians or Scythians are reputed to have brought with them the original 'aeltacht' – or Gaelic – language and culture. The Milesians' descendants, and those of subsequent invasions, split into three clans which were spread abroad.

O ne Irish clan was enslaved by the Greeks, only to escape back to Ireland and form the Fir Boig, or Bog Men, warrior tribe. Another clan settled in northern Greece, studying the art of the Druids and becoming the god-like Tuatha de Dannan, or Wise People of the Mother Goddess Danu. They, too, returned to Ireland to rule over the Fir Boig. Little is known of the fate of the third clan, but the Fir Boig eventually came face-to-face with the Tuatha De Danann, whom they defeated. However, the Tuatha made a pact with Minedh, or Nemed. They agreed to relinquish their lands to the conquerors, on condition that they should rule over the underground world.

The Celtic Tuatha, however, had supernatural powers and were able to lay a curse on the Fir, who were banished into tumuli. In Ireland today, the Fir are still believed to inhabit the Underworld in the shape of the famed 'little people'. These are the 'fairy folk', like the leprechauns, the banshee, or 'bean si' women, and the 'tipsy' cluricauns, said to be nocturnal and who are characters from the 'si', or 'sidhe', descendants of the ancient Tuatha and the Fir. Legend has it that, as late as the 5th century, the Tuatha survived the advent of Christianity by metamorphosing themselves into fairies. Even the ancient Celtic super-goddess, Brigit, who oversaw fertility, remains an integral part of these legends.

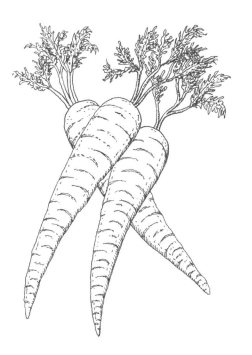

The carrot is a familiar root vegetable which mixes well with all manner of foods. Apart from its phallic shape and vibrant colour, since Classical times – and probably even before it was cultivated – the carrot was a known aphrodisiac. Containing iron, sugar, and the vitamins A, B, and C, carrots are known to restore the nervous system and assist in mentally promoting sexual activity. 'Carrot top' was once used as an expression to describe the many Irish people who had red hair, even though the top of a carrot is as green as the meadows of Ireland itself!

CARROT SOUP

10 ounces of carrots, chopped
1 large onion, sliced
2 ounces of butter
1 pint of orange juice
2 pints of chicken stock
1 teaspoon of salt and white pepper, mixed
1 teaspoon of chives, chopped
1 tablespoon of single cream

Method: *Saute the onions in half the butter until soft. Add the carrots and cook for 2 minutes. Stir in the stock and bring to the boil. Cover, then simmer for 30 minutes, or until carrots are very soft. Let it cool, then liquidize soup in a blender. In a large pan, add soup to the orange juice, then season. Heat gently and stir in the rest of the butter. When the butter has melted, serve. Garnish with cream and chopped chives.*

For over 4,000 years, Ireland's largest man-made structures were the country's famous passage tombs. Dating from a time when myth merged into mystery, one of these ancient tombs is at Knowth, on the banks of the River Boyne in Country Meath. It is said to contain the largest gallery of Neolithic art in the world. Pre-dating the pyramids of Egypt, there are three major passage tomb sites, at Knowth, Newgrange, and Dowth.

Knowth's ancient burial complex, thought to be in use around 3000BC, contains two main tombs, facing east and west, surrounded by 19 smaller burial sites. Both of the larger passages – one 1345 feet (105m) long, the other 114 feet (35m) in length – were the last resting places of more than 100 of Ireland's prehistoric Kings.

What particularly fascinates archaeologists are the finely carved decorations on the walls of the tombs at Knowth and Newgrange. The celebrated artistry of Celtic design reached its zenith with the production of the *Book of Kells*, dating from about AD400 and embellished with the typically interlocking and woven patterns of stylized flora and fauna. It is thought that the tomb decorations may reveal the origins of the book's complicated illustrations, as they consist of whorls, spirals, circles and zigzags. It is possible to trace the development of Irish Celtic art from these primitive origins, through Bronze and Iron Age artifacts. As early as 2200BC, Ireland's inhabitants were working in gold, copper and bronze, and their crescent-shaped ornaments were decorated with raised patterns not dissimilar to those found on the walls of the neolithic tombs.

By 1200BC, strips of gold were being twisted into ornaments like torcs, or necklaces and bracelets. With a little imagination, the twisted gold ornaments might be seen as the earliest form of the Celtic art based on intricately entwined animals and birds. A number of stashes of these objects have been discovered, notably the Gleninsheen gorget, made in 700BC, the 600BC Ballinesker Hoard, and the Broighter Hoard, which dates from around 100BC. One Medieval relic is the Cross of Cong, wrought in brass, silver, and a piece of wood said to have come from the True Cross. Another is an elaborately decorated 8th-century cloak pin, known as the Tara Brooch, and linked with Ireland's ancient kings. The Ardagh Chalice is from the same era, and was used in religious ceremonies. Too much of what this chalice once contained, would render you 'dankey', the Irish for 'slightly drunk'.

DANKEY STEW

2 large scrag mutton chops
2 onions, quartered
2 carrots, sliced
3 celery sticks, chopped
2 potatoes, sliced
2 ounces of pearl barley, soaked in cold water
1 tablespoon of mushroom ketchup
1 pint of Irish stout
1 teaspoon of salt and freshly ground black
pepper, mixed

Method: *Place the celery and carrots in a large casserole dish. Place the meat on top of them, followed by the onion quarters. Pour in the stout and the mushroom ketchup, then season. Finish off with layers of potato slices. Bring the mixture to the boil on the stove, then cook in a slow oven for 1 hour. Sprinkle the barley into the stew, and cook for another hour.*

Ireland's patron saint is Saint Patrick, who lived from AD389-461. It is said that he was Maewyn, the son of a Welsh deacon, and was captured by Irish raiders led by King Niall. He then spent six years in Ireland as a young slave, working as a shepherd in County Antrim. Eventually, he escaped to France, where he spent 20 years studying in monasteries – until a vision ordered him to take Christianity to the Irish. It is said that Saint Patrick used the trefoil leaves of the shamrock to explain the idea of the Holy Trinity to Ireland's countryfolk. It is also claimed that it was he who drove all the snakes from Irish soil, and that when he died, he was buried in Downpatrick, County Down.

A bell, said to have belonged to St Patrick, resides in Dublin's National Museum. St Patrick's Day falls on March 17th, although it has only been celebrated as a public holiday since 1901. Because of the saint's time working as a sheep herder – and as a shepherd in the Christian sense – St Patrick has always been portrayed holding a shepherd's crook. Also for this reason, Ireland's national dish is based on mutton.

Parsley is a classic Irish herb, used in a number of country dishes. Nicholas Culpeper, the famous early 17th-century herbalist, wrote three entire pages on the benefits of parsley, which had been introduced from southern Europe during the previous century.

TRADITIONAL IRISH STEW

2 pounds of mutton, scrag-end and neck,
chopped in pieces
3 onions, sliced
4 carrots, sliced
5 potatoes cut in thick slices
2 leeks, sliced
1 tablespoon of pearl barley
1 teaspoon of fresh thyme leaves, chopped fine
2 tablespoons of plain flour
1 ounce of melted butter
1½ pints of stock
1 tablespoon of parsley, chopped fine
1 teaspoon of salt and freshly ground black
pepper, mixed

Method: *Season the flour with half the salt and pepper mix. Cut excess fat off the mutton pieces. Fry fat pieces in a casserole dish until their fat is released. Discard the fat pieces, then brown the mutton in the liquid fat. Set meat aside, leaving a quarter of it in the bottom of the dish. Place a layer of onion slices over the meat in the dish. Follow this with a layer of carrots, then a layer of leeks. Season, then add one layer of potatoes and another layer of meat. Continue layers and seasoning. Sprinkle last layer of meat with thyme. Add the parsley, pearl barley and the stock, then finish off with a layer of potatoes. Pour melted butter over the top layer. Replace on stove, bring to a simmer, then skim off any scum. Bring to the boil, then cover the casserole with its lid. Boil for 3 minutes, then turn down and simmer for around 2 hours until cooked.*
Parsley dumplings (see following recipe) complement this recipe perfectly. After cooking the stew, the meat and vegetables are removed and kept warm, whilst the dumplings are cooked in the boiling liquid.

PARSLEY DUMPLINGS

4 ounces of self-raising flour
2 ounces of shredded suet
1 tablespoon of fresh parsley, chopped fine
1 teaspoon of salt and freshly ground black
pepper, mixed

Method: *In a bowl, mix the flour with the parsley, salt and pepper. Lightly mix in the suet. Add a little water, mixing until the dough is stiff. Mould into eight dumpling balls. Bring the liquid from the Irish Stew to the boil and place dumplings in it. Cover the pan and continue boiling for around 25 minutes. Serve with the stew and the liquid.*

Known as the 'Land of Saints and Scholars', Ireland's panoply of saints, and their holy places, are all wreathed in extraordinary myths and folk tales. Croagh Patrick, known locally as the 'Reek', in County Mayo, is Ireland's holy mountain. It is here, allegedly, that St Patrick fasted for 40 days during Lent, in the year AD411. The 45 public houses in Westport, the nearest town to the Reek, are testament to the thousands of thirsty pilgrims who pass through here to climb the sacred mountain. This beautiful Georgian town was first laid out in 1780, by James Wyatt. Up on Croagh Patrick, a statue of the saint dominates the skyline.

Veal comes from two- to three-month-old calves which have been especially fed on milk. It is a tender, pink, firm flesh, and a noted delicacy. There are eight different cuts of veal, from cutlets and loin, to shoulder and breast, and from middle neck to knuckle, and scrag end to the fillet, used in the following recipe. The thin, tender escalopes, cut from the leg of the calf, are the most popular and tastiest part of the animal. Probably the finest veal in Ireland comes from County Kerry, where the Kerry breed of cattle is a native of south-west Ireland and is rarely seen elsewhere. There is a proverb in the counties of Kerry and Donegal: 'Kerry cows know Sunday'. This refers to the tradition of taking blood from the cows, which was boiled into a mixture with sorrel to produce a thick, wholesome broth for Sunday's lunch, if the peasant folk had no other food available.

Right: Veal Coddle.

VEAL CODDLE

6 veal escalopes
1 ounce of stewing veal
2 ounces of cooked ham
4 ounces of pork sausage meat
1 garlic clove, crushed
1 egg yolk, beaten
1½ tablespoons of plain flour
1 ounce of butter
½ teaspoon of salt and freshly ground black pepper, mixed

For the First Sauce:
1 onion, chopped fine
1½ ounces of butter
1 pound of tinned tomatoes
1 garlic clove crushed
½ teaspoon of salt and pepper, mixed

For the Second Sauce:
2 ounces of hard Irish cheese, grated
1 teaspoon of arrowroot
½ teaspoon of turmeric
1 pint of cream

Method: *Beat the veal escalopes flat. Mince together the stewing veal, cooked ham and sausage meat. Stir in the salt, pepper and garlic. Make six sausage shapes with the mixture and roll one inside each escalope. Tie each roll with cooking string. Dip each roll into egg yolk, then flour, to coat. Fry the rolls in the butter for 15 minutes until golden brown. Cook rolls in a dish, in a moderate oven, for a further 10 minutes. For the first sauce, cook the onion in butter, then add the other ingredients. Reduce for 10 minutes. For the second sauce, mix all the ingredients together and heat them slowly, stirring all the time. Remove the string from the rolls. Pour the first sauce, then the second sauce over the rolls. Brown rolls under the grill.*

The twentieth century is peppered with literary Irish gems, including those of Sean O'Casey (1884-1964), whose trilogy, *Shadow of a Gunman*, *Juno and the Paycock*, and *The Plough and the Stars*, was penned about the Dublin slums where he was brought up. Samuel Beckett (1906-1989) was one of Dublin's leading playwrights, famous for his trilogy, *Molloy/Malone Dies/The Unnamable*, *Waiting for Godot*, and *Endgame*. Another Irish literary luminary was Brendan Behan (1923-1964), with his fine works like *The Hostage*, *The Borstal Boy*, and *The Quare Fellow*, set in Dublin's notorious Mountjoy Prison. Behan is buried in the city's Glasnevin (or Prospect) Cemetery. Then there is the work of Seamus Heaney, born in 1939, and considered the finest Irish poet since W B Yeats. His more famous works include *Sweeny Astray*, *Death of a Naturalist*, *Selected Poems*, *Station Island*, *Seeing Things*, *North* (published in 1975), *Field Work* (1979) and *The Haw Lantern* (published in 1987).

The celebrated author, Anthony Trollope, spent several years in Ireland and set his 1844 novel, *The Kellys and O'Kellys*, in the village of Dunmore, in Connacht. The following year, the Great Potato Famine hit the island's peasantry. In this book, he vividly describes the Irish country kitchen, comparing it to the "most orderly" English kitchen. He writes, "The difference of the English and Irish character is nowhere more plainly discerned than in their respective kitchens." Apart from references to the occupants of the Irish kitchen – two pigs, a cockerel, three or four chickens, a dog and a heap of potatoes – Trollope says "an Irish kitchen is devoted to hospitality in every sense of the word."

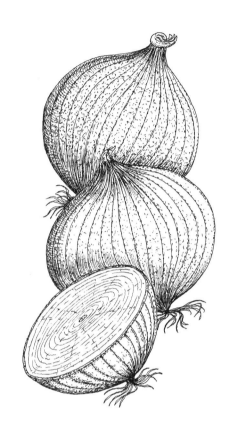

All forms of onions (Allium cepa), like scallions, shallots and leeks, including the red onions, Spanish onions and the ordinary white onion, are essential ingredients for many Irish dishes. Medicinally, onions are considered good for asthma, coughs and colds, and have an antiseptic quality.

BACON & CABBAGE STEW

1 medium-sized cabbage, shredded

4 rashers of streaky bacon, chopped

1 pound of pork sausages, sliced in chunks

1 apple, peeled, cored and chopped

1 shallot, or small onion, chopped fine

2 ounces of butter

3 pints of stock

1 bay leaf

1 teaspoon of salt and freshly ground black pepper, mixed

Method: *Melt the butter in a pan and cook the cabbage in it for 15 minutes. Add the stock, salt and pepper, shallot and bay leaf. Simmer for around 30 minutes until the cabbage is tender. Add the bacon and sausages and simmer for 10 more minutes. Add the apple and continue simmering for a further 15 minutes. Remove the bay leaf and serve hot.*

The Dublin Coddle recipe which follows was a favourite of Jonathan Swift (1667-1745). He was born in Dublin and educated at Trinity College. He left Ireland for England in 1688. On his return to Ireland, his first works were published in 1704. After editing the *Examiner* from 1710-1711, he became Dean of St Patrick's Cathedral, Dublin, in 1713, a post which he held until his death. In *The Conduct of the Allies*, Swift wrote, "It is folly of too many to mistake the echo of a London coffee-house for the voice of the kingdom." This was a comment on the trivial treatment of Ireland by the elite of London. After the publication of *The Drapier's Letters*, about a Dublin tailor and, later, *Gulliver's Travels* in 1726, Swift suffered a brain disease and gradually sank into insanity.

DUBLIN CODDLE

8 thick slices of ham, cut into chunks
16 pork chipolatas
4 large onions, chopped
2 pounds of sliced potatoes
4 tablespoons of chopped parsley
½ teaspoon of salt
½ teaspoon of ground black pepper

Method: *Boil the ham and chipolatas in water for 5 minutes. Strain off the liquid and save it. Put the ham and sausages in a casserole dish. Layer with potatoes, onions and parsley, seasoning the layers with salt and pepper. Cover ingredients with the saved stock. Put on the casserole lid, then cook on a high heat for 30 minutes. Remove the cover and cook until the liquid has reduced by half.*

During the 1845-48 Great Irish Famine, soup kitchens proliferated throughout the country. Many people relied entirely on their daily quota of this free soup for survival when their potato crops were hit by the blight. It was Alexis Soyer, the chef at London's Reform Club, in Pall Mall, who devised the ingredients and wrote the official recipe for the universally dispensed soup. During 1848 alone, a total of 8,750 souls were sustained each day on Soyer's soup.

Right: Bacon, Beef & Bean Coddle.

BACON, BEEF & BEAN CODDLE

8 ounces of dried white beans, soaked overnight
1 tablespoon of vegetable oil
2 ounces of streaky bacon, cut into small squares
8 ounces of shin of beef, diced
2 bay leaves
2 field mushrooms, chopped
3 teaspoons of ground cumin
1 onion, finely chopped
3 cloves of garlic, chopped
3 sticks of celery, chopped
2 carrots, chopped
3 tomatoes, blanched, peeled and chopped
2 tablespoons of malt vinegar
2 pints of stock
Pinch of salt and black pepper

Method: *Rinse the beans thoroughly. Cover them with the stock and boil for 10 minutes. Heat the oil in a large, heavy pot and saute the bacon, beef, bay leaves, cumin, onion, garlic, celery and carrots. Add the mushrooms, beans and the stock, tomatoes, vinegar, and seasoning. Bring to the boil. Reduce the heat, cover and simmer for 1½ hours, or until the meat is tender. Remove the bay leaves and serve hot.*

The cookery of a nation is just as much part of its customs and traditions as are its laws and language.'

'A Book of Food', P Morton Shand (1929)

Chapter Four

COLCANNON & CHAMP

In the north-west of Ireland, at the hill of Ushnagh, County Westmeath, the local harvest festival is called the 'Lughnasa'. It is named after its founder, Lugh, a mythical warrior who was condemned to death by his tyrant grandfather, Balar, on his birth. A local smith, Goibhniu, took the child away and reared him. Balar was endowed with a magical eye which would transfix all his opponents. However, when Lugh eventually met his grandfather in battle, he shot out the evil eye before it could slay him. Lugh went on to fulfil the office of a panoply of gods because of his legendary skills, and had the honour of becoming the wisest of the wise. At that time, evil creatures known as Fomoiri occupied the island and subjugated its inhabitants. The King of Ireland asked Lugh to organise the battle in which the Fomoiri were finally routed from the country. There are countless tales in Irish folklore about the earth and its produce, particularly as many peasants once survived solely on root vegetables. Many of these legends go back into pre-history and involve mysterious deities responsible for the fertility of the land, such as the benefactorial Brighid, or Brigit.

Brighid, or Saint Brigit, was the patroness of children and animals. She was the Irish goddess of the hearth and fire, and therefore important in the continuation of traditional cooking. St Brigit also presided over poetry and handicrafts, and the cross of St Brigit – fashioned from rushes and straw – can still be seen, hanging from the walls of many rural cottage in Ireland.

The three sister goddesses or legendary Queens of Tuatha De Dannan, Banba, Fotla and Eire Danaan, also represented the spirit of Ireland in their poetry and literary skills. It was Eire Danaan who gave her name to modern Ireland (Eire), and all three are said to be buried in a mound at Carnfree, County Roscommon. Brighid was one of the many deities in Irish folklore, which mingled local tales with those of the Norsemen, Vikings, and the Gauls. In Gallic legends, the master of the universe was named Taranis. It was he who was responsible for the rain which fed the earth and made the crops grow. However, for his bounty, Taranis demanded the awful price of human sacrifice. Similarly, the Gallic warrior deity, Teutates, also demanded that his victims be drowned. Donn Firinne, in Munster, is the home of the Irish ancestor-god, and is said to be the destination of all Irish people when they die.

Right: It was Taranis, the master of the universe in Gallic legends, who was responsible for the rain which fed the earth and made the crops grow.

THE STORY OF POTATOES

Potatoes were first cultivated, thousands of years before the arrival of Europeans, by the ancient Incas who lived in the high Andes mountains of South America. They used to preserve the potatoes by leaving them out in the the hot sun, and during the frosty nights. This dehydrated the tubers, or freeze-dried them into a form called 'chuno'. The cold climate and damp atmosphere of their original home, around the shores of Lake Titicaca, was very similar to that of Ireland, which is why potatoes took so well to the Irish soil. For some reason, the early Spanish naturalists who first came across the potato, combined its name with that of the Caribbean sweet potato, or 'batatas', hence the word 'potato'.

Some historians suggest that it was the naval Admiral and first slave-trader, Sir John Hawkins, who first introduced potatoes to England in 1563. It was reputedly Sir Walter Raleigh who first brought them to Ireland from his colony in Virginia, USA, in the 1580s. Raleigh was appointed Mayor of Youghal, in County Cork, until he fell out of favour with Queen Elizabeth I. Upon her death, in 1603, and by the order of King James, Raleigh was imprisoned in the Tower of London, later to be beheaded by the axe – a fate which he ruefully called "A sharp medicine, but an infallible cure!" In 1580, Sir Walter Raleigh met the famous poet, Edmund Spenser (1552-1599), at Castle Matrix, in County Limerick, where he presented him with his tubers from the New World. Spenser not only went on to cultivate the first potatoes in

Ireland, but penned his famous six books, known as *Faerie Queene,* there. Raleigh also gave some potatoes to Lord Southwell, who went on to devise the open-field method of land cultivation in Ireland. The annual Walter Raleigh Potato Festival is still held in Youghal. After its introduction, the potato became a staple diet in Ireland during the 17th and 18th centuries because, under British rule, the wealth of Irish dairy produce and cereals were reserved for export to the United Kingdom.

Although the potato was adopted by the Irish, it was not until the bad northern European grain harvests of the late-17th, and 18th centuries, that the potato became accepted in England. Potatoes were so easy to grow in Ireland's rich soil, that they soon dominated the local vegetable plots. Even as early as the first Irish famines of the early 1740s, Edmund Burke wrote, "Whoever travels through this kingdom will see such poverty as few nations in Europe can equal." By the early 19th century, half of Ireland's peasantry had forsaken traditional cultivation and were almost entirely dependent on the potato. Indeed, many poor people ate nothing else. Ireland was one of the most densely populated countries in Europe by 1845, with eight million people. During 1847 – the last year of the Great

Potato Famine – over 250,000 people died of starvation when the main crop, potatoes, failed for the third disastrous year. Because of the potato blight that struck their staple diet between 1845-47, millions of Irish people emigrated to North America, the place from which the potato had been introduced. Dependent on potatoes, the Irish vainly looked to England to provide an alternative staple diet for the starving population. All they were offered was a maize meal, a corn flour coincidentally made from the American maize corn cob. The following recipe is included here because of its historical connection with potatoes, as countless lives were saved by making bread with the yellow (pronounced 'yaller') corn flour.

YALLER SPOTTED DOG

1 pound of plain flour
1 pound of maize meal
1 teaspoon of sugar
1 teaspoon of salt
1 teaspoon of bicarbonate of soda
5 tablespoons of buttermilk
1 tablespoon of milk
1 pound of sultanas

Method: *Sift the flour, maize meal, soda, salt and sugar together. Stir in buttermilk until the mixture becomes tacky. Turn mixture onto a floured board and knead in the sultanas. Mould the mixture into a round, flat cake. Cut a cross on the top of the cake, then brush milk over the top to form a glaze. Bake in a moderate oven for around 45 minutes. The cake should be done when the bottom sounds hollow when tapped. Serve while still warm with lots of butter.*

Black pepper is produced by grinding the dried, unripe fruit of an Indian climbing vine, (Piper nigram), or the peppercorns. The colour comes from the pericarp (shells) of the tiny fruits, which turns black when dried. When the unripe, green peppercorns ripen, they turn red and are harvested. They are then shelled and ground to make white pepper. Pepper acts as an internal cooling agent and has a settling effect on the stomach. It also stimulates the appetite, making it an important cooking condiment. For the most pungent flavour, black pepper should be freshly ground, as and when it is needed. The quantity used is a matter of taste, and all seasoning quantities given in these recipes are suggestions only. The potato soup recipe that follows is greatly improved by the liberal use of black pepper.

BASIC POTATO SOUP

2 pounds of potatoes, peeled and sliced
1 carrot, peeled and sliced
2 onions, sliced
2 ounces of butter
2 tablespoons of cream
2 pints of stock
1 pint of milk
1 bay leaf
1 teaspoon of fresh parsley, chopped
½ teaspoon of thyme
1 tablespoon of chives, chopped fine
1 teaspoon each of salt and black pepper

Method: *In a large pan, sweat the onions in the butter until translucent. Add the potatoes and sliced carrot, then stir in the stock and milk. Add the bay leaf, parsley, thyme, salt and pepper. Simmer on a gentle heat for around 1 hour, then remove the bay leaf. Liquidize the soup in a blender, then return it to the pan on the stove. Re-heat and serve, garnishing each bowl of soup with chives and a swirl of cream.*

William Butler Yeats (1865-1939) was probably Ireland's most notable poet, although he made his name only after moving to London. Yeats' best-known works include *Crossways*, written in 1889, *In the Seven Woods* (1904), *Collected Poems, Fairy and Folk Tales of Ireland*, and *September 1913*. In 1928, Yeats was awarded the Nobel Prize for Literature, becoming a Free State senator between 1922 and 1928, when *The Tower* was published. Yeats helped to found the world's first national theatre, The Abbey, in Dublin. Later, in 1932, he established the Irish Academy of Letters. *Last Poems* was published posthumously in 1939, the year of his death. He is buried in Drumcliff churchyard, County Sligo, where he spent his boyhood.

IRISH POTATO CAKES

1½ pounds of cooked potatoes
3 tablespoons of plain flour
2 ounces of salted butter
1 teaspoon of salt
½ teaspoon of freshly ground black pepper

Method: *While the potatoes are still hot from cooking, place them in a bowl. Add half the butter, the salt and pepper, then mash them together. Mix in the flour. Turn the mixture out onto a floured surface. Shape the mixture into 8 balls. Flatten them slightly, then coat them in flour. Melt the remaining ounce of butter in a large frying pan. Fry the potato cakes until golden on both sides, drain on kitchen paper and serve while hot.*

There are several hundred varieties of potatoes grown throughout the world, and the white Irish variety of potatoes (solanum tuberosum) are said to be among the sweetest and fluffiest anywhere. Arguably, the best new potatoes in Ireland are the Comer variety, from County Down. The versatility of the potato, whether new or old, gave rise to a wealth of imaginative ways of cooking this vegetable. Potatoes are almost 80% water, with about 2% protein. They store riboflavin, niacin and thiamin in – and just below – their skins. They also contain vitamins B and C, and have some mineral content, like iron and potassium. An average baked potato provides the recommended daily intake of all these essentials. It offers the most easily assimilated form of starch and contains little fat or salt.

In the early days of its cultivation, a special – usually three-legged – iron pot was reserved for potato boiling. Traditional Irish pancakes, the recipe for which follows, were once served as a main meal. These days, however, they are more usually served to accompany meat.

IRISH PANCAKES

3 potatoes, boiled
3 tablespoons of plain flour
1 egg, beaten
2 tablespoons of butter, melted
1 teaspoon of cooking soda
1 teaspoon of salt
4 tablespoons of buttermilk

Method: *Mash, or press the well-boiled potatoes through a strainer. Leave to cool. With a fork, mix the melted butter into the potatoes. Stir in the beaten egg, flour and salt. Mix the cooking soda into the buttermilk. Add this mixture to the potato mix. Butter a hot griddle. Drop the mixture, a tablespoon at a time, onto the griddle. Brown the pancakes on both sides, repeating until all of the mixture is used.*

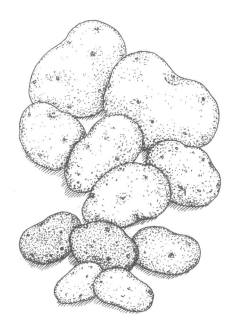

Right: the white Irish variety of potatoes (solanum tuberosum) are said to be among the sweetest and fluffiest anywhere.

POTATO SCONES

1 pound of potatoes
3 ounces of butter
4 ounces of plain flour
2 teaspoons of salt

Method: *Boil the potatoes for about 20 minutes, until soft. Mash them with the salt and half of the butter. Work the flour into the mashed potato until it is stiff. Turn mix out onto a floured board. Roll out, then divide into 10 equal pieces. Roll the pieces into balls, then flatten them out. Fry the scones in the remaining butter. Brown on each side and serve hot with butter.*

Ireland has a wealth of architectural monuments and places which link the country with many famous people and events. In Stabane, the Gray's Printing Works was the place where John Dunlop, printer of the American Declaration of Independence, studied. Handel played on the organ in Saint Michan's Church, Dublin. Sir Christopher Wren is said to have designed the Main Guard building in Clonmel, while Augustus Welby Pugin, architect of Westminster's Houses of Parliament details, designed the Cathedral of Saint Mary in Killarney. The park in Eyre Square, Galway, is now a memorial to President Kennedy, as is County Wexford's John F Kennedy Arboretum. Just outside Omagh is the Ulster American Folk Park, tracing 200 years of Irish emigration to America. Ireland is also no stranger to Hollywood, as *Ryan's Daughter* and *Far and Away* were filmed in Dingle, *The Field* was shot in Killarney Harbour and *The Quiet Man* was made in Cong village. Cong was visited by President Ronald Reagan, himself a famous Hollywood actor before he became a politician.

O'BRIEN'S POTATOES

4 potatoes, boiled
1 leek, sliced and boiled
2 onions, chopped fine
2 tablespoons of plain flour
4 ounces of mature Irish cheese, grated
2 ounces of dry brown breadcrumbs
6 tablespoons of hot milk
2 ounces of butter
Pinch of salt
Pinch of cayenne pepper

Method: *Slice the cooked potatoes and mix with the cooked leeks, raw onion, flour and salt. Mix in the milk and three quarters of the cheese. Grease a baking dish, then pour in mixture. Sprinkle the top of the mix with breadcrumbs, then the remaining cheese. Dot pieces of the butter all over the dish, then sprinkle with cayenne. Cook in a moderate oven until the top browns and bubbles. Serve while still piping hot.*

Religious monuments dot the Irish countryside and many date from Saint Patrick's missionary arrival in Ireland in the 5th century AD. Dating from the same century is St Patrick's round tower, near Killala Cathedral and the 'ogham stone', inscribed in Gaelic, at Ardfert. The 6th-century 'beehive' cell attributed to St Finan is at Waterville, and there are those attributed to the 5th-century St Seanach on the Magharee Islands, while more examples are found at Great Skellig rock, off the west coast. There is also St Kevin's 6th-century monastic settlement in Glendalough, and that of St Declan, dating from the 7th century, at Ardmore. The 8th-century Inscribed Stone at Kilnasaggart is said to be the oldest datable Christian monument.

Saffron was first brought to England by a pilgrim, during the reign of Edward III, in the mid-1300s, and it was grown extensively in places like Saffron Walden, in Essex. At this time, saffron was such an important commodity that anyone caught adulterating it could expect to receive the death penalty. The spice's importance died out in most of England except Cornwall, where it is still commonly used. Saffron possibly arrived in Cornwall with the Phoenician traders, and it may have been from Cornwall, in the days of King Mark, who was betrothed to Isolde, the daughter of an Irish King, that saffron came to Ireland. The delicate, orange-red stamens are collected from the saffron crocus (Crocus stavius) and dried to make this powerful colouring agent, used particularly in rice dishes and paellas. Because the stamens must be picked by hand, saffron is the most expensive spice in the world. It takes around 30,000 stamens to produce just half a pound of saffron. While saffron is prized for its particular, delicate flavour, the much cheaper turmeric may be substituted.

SAFFRON POTATOES

2 pounds of potatoes
1 pound of hard Irish cheese, grated
4 tablespoons of cream
4 tablespoons of mutton stock
1½ ounces of butter
3 stamens of saffron
1 teaspoon of freshly ground black pepper

Method: *Boil the peeled potatoes until tender. Strain, allow to cool, then slice the potatoes thinly. Place a layer of slices in a buttered baking dish. Cover the layer with a little cheese and a sprinkling of pepper. Repeat until all the potatoes are used, reserving a tablespoon of cheese. Soak the saffron in a little boiling water. Mix the stock, cream and remaining cheese with the saffron and now-yellow water. Pour the mixture over the top potato layer. Bake in a moderate oven for 20 minutes. Saffron Potatoes make an ideal accompaniment to the Stout-Braised Beef recipe on page 72.*

> *By noone see your dinner, be readie and neate,*
> *let meate tarrie servant, not servant his meate.'*
>
> Thomas Tusser (circa 1524-1580)

APPLE AND POTATO SALAD

1 red apple, peeled and cored

1 pound of new potatoes

2 sprigs of fresh mint

1 egg yolk

1 teaspoon of mixed mustard

½ pint of vegetable oil

1 tablespoon of cider

4 rashers of bacon, lightly grilled and cut in strips

½ lettuce, divided into leaves

3 teaspoons of lemon juice

½ teaspoon of salt

½ teaspoon of freshly ground black pepper

Method: *Make the salad by boiling new potatoes in salted water with 2 mint sprigs. When tender, drain, cool, peel and quarter the potatoes. Slice the apple into segments and sprinkle them with lemon juice. Make mayonnaise by beating mustard into the egg yolk. Very slowly, whisk in the oil a little at a time, until the mixture thickens. Once all the oil is all mixed in, stir in the cider. Add the salt and pepper and stir again. Toss the apple and potatoes in the mayonnaise. Serve chilled on lettuce leaves, garnished with bacon pieces.*

Ireland is famous for its glorious variety of religious edifices, many of which date from the 13th century and earlier. Two of the oldest Christian sites are the AD545 monastic site of Clonmacnoise, founded by St Ciaran, and St Finian's Abbey on Valentia Island, established in AD560. There is also the 1000-year-old Gallarus Oratory, one of the best-preserved Christian churches in the country, and the 10th-century Romanesque chapel on the Rock of Cashel – one of the finest examples in Europe and site of the enthronement of Ireland's ancient Kings. The Round Tower at St Declan's monastic site was built in the 12th century and is one of the best-preserved bell towers of its type. In the grounds of the 12th-century Abbeyleix Abbey, there is the 13th-century Monk's Bridge. St Multose's Church in Kinsale dates from the 13th century, as does the Dominican Priory at Athenry. Christopher Columbus is said to have prayed at the 14th-century Church of St Nicholas, in Galway. The Carmelite Friary at Loughrea, nearby, dates from the same period.

'Health to thee, good apple-tree,

Well to bear pocket-fulls,

hat-fulls,

Peck-fulls, bushel-bag fulls.'

Apple orchard harvest rhyme

Although many of Ireland's ancient churches are now in ruins, they still retain their grandeur, and lend a haunting beauty to the landscape. One example is Jerpoint Abbey in the south-east, founded in 1158. Another, in the west of the country, is the 12th-century ruin of St Finan's Church, which stands in the middle of Lough Currane. In Ardfert, one can see the ruins of the 13th-century St Brendan's Cathedral, and the remains of a Franciscan friary from the same era.

Another ruined Franciscan friary is the 12th-century Grey Abbey at Kildare. At Ballinskellig are the ruins of an Augustine abbey, while at Wexford there is a 12th-century Augustine priory. It was here, at Selskar Abbey, that King Henry II did penance for the murder of Thomas A'Becket in 1172. Aligo Abbey and Rathfern Abbey are 13th-century Dominican sites, as is the friary at Roscommon and the priory at Newtownards. This, and the 10th-century cathedral are on the Ardmore peninsula, near to the Curragh, where the famous horse races are held.

Just as there are 'horses for courses', as every Irishman and woman knows, there are potatoes for recipes. Comer Potatoes from County Cown are probably best for Colcannon, traditionally served at a family feast. Silver coins or little charms are hidden in this dish, to be discovered by the children. This practice mirrors that of English cooks, who would hide small silver coins in the traditional Christmas, or Plum Pudding. This form of colcannon will be a beautiful, pale green colour, because of the addition of kale, a local crop, which is cooked in the same way as cabbage. Other versions of colcannon include onions instead of leeks, and include parsnips, or white cabbage.

COLCANNON

1 pound of potatoes, boiled
1 pound of curly kale, sliced
1 large leek, sliced thin
1 pint of single cream
3 ounces of butter, melted
½ teaspoon of salt
½ teaspoon freshly ground black pepper

Method: *Cook the kale in a little water for about 10 minutes. When soft, chop the kale leaves finely. Stew the leek slices in the cream until soft. Mash the potatoes into the leeks and cream. Beat the kale into the mixture. Put the mixture into a pan and heat gently, whisking thoroughly. Add salt and pepper to taste. Spoon the warm mixture into a deep serving dish. Make a well in the centre of the mixture. Pour the melted butter into the well and serve.*

Champ, also known in some localities as 'stelk', can be made in a communal casserole dish, or in individual dishes. This is very similar to colcannon, and is a version of the traditional 'coiblide', where onions replace the spring onions. Chives or shallots are often substituted for spring onions, and parsley is sometimes added to basic champ. Other recipes include carrots, which are pre-cooked in milk, peas, and even nettles. As with colcannon, a spoon is used to take the champ from the outside of the dish and to dip it into the melted butter in the centre, before eating.

IRISH CHAMP

8 potatoes, boiled and mashed
4 ounces of spring onions, chopped
4 ounces of butter
½ pint of milk
1 teaspoon of salt and pepper, mixed

Method: *Boil the spring onions in the milk, simmering them until tender. Mix the milk and spring onions into the mashed potato. Spoon the hot mixture into 8 ramekin dishes. Make an indentation in the centre of each dish. Cut the butter into 8, then place one piece of butter in each of the hollows. Sprinkle a little salt and pepper on each dish, then serve as the butter is melting.*

Chapter Five

VEGETARIAN BAKES

Right down through the ages, the Celtic bards, or story-tellers, related the tales of tribal feats, the chieftains' victories, and legends of mythical characters. These bards, who also made up poems, and might be accompanied by a harp or flute player, would take an apprenticeship of up to 12 years to learn the stories and legends by heart. They were known as 'fili', and were in such demand that they were paid for their efforts in gold. Filis were always the centre of attention, and the skills of their poetry reflected the importance of the clan's lord, chieftain, or ruler.

Irish poetry has its roots in the dark mists of time, and the tales that were told in rhyme were as convoluted and intricately woven as the art of the ancient Celts. The tradition of story-telling and poetry has haunted Ireland and bewitched generations for many millennia, and has not been watered down by the passing of years. In the 1600s there was a dearth of poets, who continued the tradition of being close to the aristocracy, singing the clan lords' praises in poems called 'ranns' and composing ditties around their achievements. One famous rann, rewritten by Jonathan Swift, is the tale of *O'Rourke's Feast*, about a powerful chieftain of the 1500s. The name for an Irish chieftain was 'flaith', from which the surname O'Flaherty derives.

Over the years, even the bards' surnames reflected their profession. The name Macaward, or Ward, comes from the Celtic word for bard, and O'Canty derives from the Gaelic 'cainteach', meaning a satirist. One family of poets, the O'Dalys, are able to trace their professional ancestry back to Dalach, a 7th-century disciple of St Colman.

A tale is told of one such satirist being hurled from a cliff by an irate Cromwellian invader. The soldier, goaded by the poet's witty words, cried "Sing your rann now, little man!" as he threw him to his death. When the English arrived, the Irish aristocracy was brought low and, with them, their poets and bards.

Right: at Harvest Festival time Irish tables are laden with fine country produce.

As many of the Irish aristocracy fled from the English, leaving their Irish lands and bards behind them, the bards were reduced from their elevated positions to work in the fields. Thus, the fate of high Irish culture fell from the realms of power, to be relegated into the custody of the Irish peasantry. However, the Irish still retain two poetic words for their homeland, 'Banbha', and 'Fodla'.

One celebrated 17th-century Irish poet, David O'Bruadair, famously bemoaned his fate as a labourer, but was just one of many bards who were compelled to till the soil instead of composing imaginative and evocative tales. Still, the peasants maintained their tradition of story telling and composing poetry over the hearths of their turf fires, and pitiful fare of potatoes.

Rarely, the potato pot was elaborated by the addition of buttermilk or, even more scarce, a whey made with buttermilk and sweet milk, or skimmed milk, known as 'troander'. Traditionally, buttermilk, sometimes called 'Bonny clobber' and widely used in Irish cookery, might be substituted for the milk in this age-old recipe. Parsnips are a common winter vegetable in Ireland, and improve with the first frosts. Parsnips are often grown in trenches, known as clamps.

Bay, or Bay Laurel (Laurus nobilis), was one of the earliest herbs to be used in Europe. As well as its culinary usages, bay leaves are an appetite stimulator, as are the crushed, or infused berries. Bay leaves are a narcotic, an excitant, and are used in cures for colic and hysteria. The oil in bay leaves and berries has a warm, penetrating aroma and is used in perfumes. Caulifower should be cooked with a few bay leaves as it counteracts the vegetable's tendency to become slightly bitter when cooked.

Irish Cauliflower Cheese

1 large cauliflower head, stripped of its green leaves
1 large onion, sliced
2 scallions, sliced fine
2 tomatoes, skinned and sliced
1 ounce of plain flour
6 ounces of hard Irish cheese, grated
4 eggs, separated into yolks and whites
1 pint of milk
2 tablespoons of fresh breadcrumbs
4 bay leaves
1 teaspoon of mixed mustard
½ teaspoon of salt
½ teaspoon of freshly ground black pepper

Method: *Break the cauliflower head into florettes, cutting out the stem. Steam the caulifower over boiling water with bay, till al dente. Saute the onions (but not scallions) in half of the butter until soft. Add the tomatoes and cook for 3 minutes. Make a roux by melting remaining butter and stirring in the flour. Add the milk, mustard, 4 ounces of the cheese, and the seasoning. Place the caulifower in a baking dish. Pour the tomato mix over the cauliflower, coating it with the sauce. Beat the egg whites until stiff, then place four dollops on the sauce. Make a well in each dollop, then fill each one with an egg yolk. Scatter the breadcrumbs over the dish, then the rest of the cheese. Sprinkle the scallion slices over the top and grill until golden brown.*

POTATO & PARSNIP BAKE

1 pound of potatoes, sliced
1 large onion, sliced
1 pound of parsnips, sliced
1 pint of milk or buttermilk
2 ounces of butter
1 teaspoon of salt and freshly ground black
pepper, mixed

Method: *Grease a baking dish and arrange the sliced vegetables in alternating layers of potatoes, onions and parsnips, dotting each layer with a little butter. Season each layer with salt and pepper. Make the final layer with potatoes. Pour the buttermilk over the bake. Cover the dish, and bake for 1½ hours. Remove the cover and bake for another ½ hour to brown the potatoes.*

Turf fires are still common in the cottages out in the wilds of Ireland, and turf and peat cutters still operate, especially in the west of the country. Turf fuel production is a time-consuming job and it involves cutting the turf with a spade known as a 'slane', spreading it out on a 'turf field', footing (stacking) six turfs in a pyramid shape, ricking – which involves stacking the turfs on their sides, clamping – stacking heaps of turfs near a road or path for access and, finally, drawing the turf home to the cottage. The field work, apart from cutting, was usually done by women and children, while the drawing home of the turf fuel was by the traditional Irish horse-drawn cart, or 'carr'.

LEEK & POTATO CASSEROLE

1 pound of leeks, cut into slices two fingers wide
1 pound of potatoes, cut into thin slices.
1 ounce of butter
1 ounce of wholemeal flour
2 ounces of hard Irish cheese, grated
½ pint of milk
½ teaspoon of mustard powder
½ teaspoon of freshly ground black pepper

Method: *Steam the leek slices until they are nearly cooked. Cover the potato slices with water, bring to the boil, then simmer for 10 minutes. Melt the butter in a frying pan, then add the flour gradually, stirring it in to make a roux. Cook gently for 2 minutes, stirring. Then stir in the mustard and pepper. Drain the potatoes, then layer them with the leeks in a casserole. Pour the sauce over the vegetables and sprinkle the top with cheese. Bake in a hot oven for 25 minutes until the top has turned golden brown.*

Celeriac is best known for the nutty flavour of its bulbous roots, which are used as a vegetable. This plant also contains an essential oil which is used to flavour a salt-based seasoning. Preparations from the oil are used in treatments for asthma, bronchitis, liver diseases, and fevers. A sleep-promoting tea is also made from celeriac's seeds. Root crops like parsnips and potatoes are a staple diet in Ireland, and the lesser-known celeriac adds an exotic taste to the common mix of the two. In the vegetable mash recipe that follows, the strong celery taste of the celeriac and the sweet taste of the parsnip are complemented by the starchiness of the potatoes and the milk.

PARSNIP, CELERIAC & POTATO MASH

1 pound of potatoes, chopped roughly
1 pound of celeriac, chopped roughly
1 pound of parsnips, chopped roughly
3 ounces of butter
A generous ¼ pint of milk
1 teaspoon of mixed mustard
1 teaspoon of salt and freshly ground black
pepper, mixed

Method: *Rinse the vegetables and cover them all with cold water in a pan. Bring to the boil, then simmer until the potatoes are cooked. Drain the vegetables well, then allow them to dry. Add the milk, mustard and salt and pepper. Mash the vegetables in the pan with a masher, then a fork. Over a low heat, add the butter and stir it into the mash. Serve hot.*

The Guinness brewery at St James's Gate, in Dublin, not only produces the famous draught and bottled stout, known variously as 'the wine of the country', 'the icon of Irishness', 'the dark stuff', the 'parish priest', or 'the blonde in the black skirt', it also produces beers, lager and cider. Cider is one of the first alcoholic beverages ever to be fermented. It is thought that the art of cider-making in Ireland originated with the arrival of the Vikings, and cider quickly became more popular than the local mead. Today's Irish cider can vary from 2% to 8% alcohol.

Marjoram, used in the following recipe, is more accurately called Sweet Marjoram (Origanum magorana). It is a comforting herb, used in indigestion preparations and for tension headaches. It is also a medicine for high blood pressure and sore muscles. An ancient recipe recommends a tisane, or tea made from marjoram to prevent sea-sickness – good for fishermen! Wild marjoram (Origanum vulgare), grows naturally in Ireland, but the most commonly used is the herb garden variety (Origanum onites). As a culinary herb, it goes well with almost everything except, strangely enough, fish.

Dry August and warme,

Doth harvest no harme.'

Thomas Tusser (circa 1524-1580)

Right: Parsnip Celeriac & Potato Mash.

CIDER ONION BAKE

4 onions, halved widthwise

2 ounces of butter

4 tablespoons of Irish cider

1 teaspoon of dried thyme

1 teaspoon of fresh sage, chopped fine

1 teaspoon of dried sage and marjoram mixed.

1 teaspoon of salt and freshly ground black pepper, mixed

Method: *Melt the butter in a shallow casserole dish. Place onion halves, flat side down, in the dish. Fry them until browned. Remove dish from heat and turn onions flat side up. Sprinkle with sage and thyme, salt and pepper. Pour the cider into the dish. Cover, then bake in a moderate oven for 1 hour until tender. Spoon the liquor over the onions. Sprinkle with the sage and marjoram mixture, and serve hot.*

Time is the best story-teller, according to an early Irish saying, as apt as it is true when looking at Irish mythology and legends. It was not just the classical Gaelic and Celtic deities and celebrated bards who promoted the island's rich literary tapestry. There were also the Druids, the first of which was Amergin, author of three poems which appear in *The Book of Invasions.* The Druids were the religious leaders of the Celts, who first arrived in Ireland around 1000BC. The Druids were the Celts' mediators between the people and their vast panoply of gods and goddesses. Their goddess of poetry was the famous Brighid, whose image, by the middle of the 5th century, became Saint Brigit.

Even Shakespeare recognised the importance of Ireland's Druidic religion, personifying their god of life and death, Bile, as the legendary British king, Cymbeline. Shakespeare based the three witches in his play, *Macbeth,* on Irish legend. In mythology, the chieftain Cu Chulainn met three ugly crones cooking a magical dog over a fire on a spit of rowan wood, whilst on his way to battle. They were the human forms of the deities Badb, Macha and Anand, and were known as Ban-tuath-caecha, or, 'women blind in the left eye'.

Eloquence and wisdom were also two of the six attributes of Emer, wife of the Ulster warrior, Cu Chulainn. It is said that Chulainn was killed around AD12, yet it was over six centuries after his death before the poems and legends of that time were first written down by Cenfaeled, a casualty of the Battle of Magh Rath in AD637.

PARSNIP BAKE

1 pound of parsnips, peeled and quartered
2 tablespoons of butter
1 cup of mutton stock
Pinch of salt and black pepper
Pinch of nutmeg

Method: *Parboil the parsnips for 15 minutes. Place them in an ovenproof dish and add stock, salt, pepper and nutmeg. Dot the parsnips with pieces of the butter, then bake in a moderate oven for 30 minutes.*

Up until quite recently, the traditional Irish peasant's cabin, or cottage, was a one-roomed, turf-thatched, stone-built structure. On the bleak west coast, these were sometimes set into the ground to offer more protection from the prevailing weather. Inside, the floor was of baked earth and the focal point was the turf fire. An iron pot, used for boiling potatoes, would stand on an iron griddle. A bed stood to the right of the fire, with four roof-high posts at each corner, to which was fitted straw mats for modesty. Other furniture consisted of four posts in the floor, with wicker sides, serving as a potato bin, and, beside the bed, deal shelves were used as a dresser. There would also be a few crudely made wooden stools and a chair made of straw. To one side of the door were pegs on which to hang cloaks, the main item of clothing, and above the door was a wicker-work hen-coop. This family home would be shared by a cow, or one or more pigs. But one traveller in the Ireland of 1837 remarked that he had seen cabins so poor that there was not even one pig in them!

> **'A pot was never boiled**
>
> **by beauty.'**
>
> *Old Irish saying*

> **'May the grass grow green**
>
> **before your door.'**
>
> *Early Irish curse*

Celery was introduced into Ireland in the 17th century from the Mediterranean, where it grew wild. Celery seeds are used in tomato juice and seafood dishes, pickles, chutneys, and soups and stews. The juice of celery contains vitamins A and C. It also contains traces of calcium, manganese, sulphur, potassium and organic sodium. The plant contains an essential oil, which is used to flavour a salt-based seasoning. Preparations from the oil are used in treatments for asthma, bronchitis, liver diseases, and fevers. A sleep-promoting tea is made from the seeds, and a tonic for rheumatism is prepared from an infusion of celery seeds. The leaves and stalks are used as a vegetable, both cooked and uncooked.

BRAISED IRISH CELERY

10 stalks of celery, without the leaves, and cut in two
4 ounces of streaky bacon
1 carrot, sliced
1 onion, sliced
1 pint of chicken stock
1 bouquet garni
1 teaspoon of salt and freshly ground black pepper, mixed

Method: *Put the bacon in the bottom of a casserole dish. Add the onion and carrots, then the celery. Pour in the stock, then add the bouquet garni, salt and pepper. Bring to the boil, cover, and simmer gently for 1 hour. Serve piping hot with crubeens, the recipe for which is given on page 81.*

Right: a traditional Irish 'car' or horse-drawn cart lending a colourful rustic element to the quiet country scene.

In the beautifully peaceful Clare Glen, in County Armagh, country lanes wind seemingly aimlessly through borders of hawthorn hedgerows and marshy ditches, over trickling streams and through green valleys. Now and again, a traditional Irish 'car' or horse-drawn cart might lend a colourful rustic element to the quiet country scene. Each year, however, this idyll is shattered as crowds gather to encourage competitors to hurl large iron balls weighing 28 ounces (795g), over the hills and down the dales. Known variously as 'bullets' or 'road bowling', this sport is said to have come from Holland with the Dutch soldiers of William of Orange in 1689. Players throw the bowls along the lanes, competing for distance, and a 300-metre throw is not uncommon. The ball that covers the shortest distance is known as the 'hind bowl', and the winner's bowl is that which continues the farthest over the predetermined finishing line.

RED CABBAGE BAKE

1 small red cabbage
1 pint of red wine
¼ pint of wine vinegar
1 pint of vegetable stock
3 ounces of sugar
6 black peppercorns, crushed
1 teaspoon of fresh thyme, chopped finely
1 tablespoon of salt
2 cloves of garlic, chopped fine

Method: *Shred the cabbage thinly and sprinkle with salt. Leave overnight to go limp, then rinse and drain. Bring the wine, vinegar, stock and sugar to the boil in a pan. Add the peppercorns, thyme and garlic. Bring to the boil again, then add the cabbage and boil it for 2 minutes. Reduce the heat and simmer gently for 30 minutes. Serve hot as a vegetable, or cold with a salad.*

Chapter Six

ROASTS, SUPPERS, CRUBEENS, DRISHEEN

Numerous Irish legends relate to the country's sheep and, as Saint Patrick was once a shepherd, it is no accident that mutton forms the basis of the country's national dish, Irish Stew, and many other traditional recipes. Irish legends often mingle the early days of Christianity with pagan tales, and Ireland has two major sacred sites. One is the religious pilgrimage mountain of Croagh Patrick, in County Mayo, where St Patrick is said to have fasted for 40 days. The other is the pagan site of the citadel of Tara, in County. Meath, traditional home of the Irish warrior Kings and linked to many Druid myths. This conical hill, near Navan, was the site used every three years by the ancient kings of Ireland for the meeting of the Royal parliament. Even today the hill is a special place of pilgrimage.

One historic story relates to Cormac Mac Airt, the orphaned son of an Irish King, who was killed by the ruthless Lughaidh Mac Con, who took the throne by force. At just seven years of age, Cormac was advised by a holy Druid to visit the sacred citadel of Tara. Along the way, Cormac met a distraught woman who explained that the savage Lughaidh had killed all her flock of sheep as punishment for the fact that they had been grazing on fields reserved for the royalty. Hastening on to the Hill of Tara, the young boy attempted to confront Lughaidh, his father's murderer.

Cormac was subsequently led into the royal court, where the local warlords were gathered in the presence of Lughaidh, the self-appointed king. He explained the plight of the shepherdess whom he had met on the road. Cormac suggested that the appropriate punishment, if the woman's sheep had indeed grazed the king's land, would be to take the fleece from the flock, rather than their lives, in exchange for every time the sheep grazed the royal land. The assembled company were so impressed by the boy's wisdom that they deposed the usurper Lughaidh, crowning the young Cormac as their king instead. Thus the young, precociously wise Cormac regained the throne and the rightful inheritance which the wicked Lughaidh had so cruelly taken from his father, simply with the aid of a flock of local Irish sheep and not a little Irish 'blarney', or clever talk.

Right: numerous Irish legends relate to the country's sheep.

One species of oregano (Origanum onites), a branch of the marjoram family, is more commonly known as pot marjoram, but it is wild marjoram which is more commonly called oregano. It is generally used with tomatoes and meat sauces, and can be used to flavour strong, closely-textured fish. Sweet Marjoram (Origanum magorana) is a comforting herb, used in preparations for indigestion and for tension headaches. It is also a medicine for high blood pressure, indigestion, and sore muscles.

Mutton Pot Roast

3-pound leg of mutton
1 onion, sliced
2 celery sticks, sliced
4 carrots, halved
1 pound of new potatoes
6 tablespoons of mutton stock
2 tablespoons of maize oil
1 teaspoon of salt and freshly ground black
pepper, mixed

Stuffing
8 ounces of sausage meat
1 onion, chopped
1 tablespoon of fresh parsley, chopped fine
2 teaspoons of dried oregano
1 garlic clove, crushed

Method: *Make the stuffing by mixing ingredients thoroughly in a bowl. Bone the mutton leg and stuff the cavity with stuffing. Heat the oil in a casserole and brown the leg all over. Add vegetables and stock, then season with salt and pepper. Cover casserole and cook in a low oven for 2 hours. When the mutton is tender, slice and serve with vegetables.*

For years, the tales of the Celts were handed down by word of mouth, as the Druids, or pagan priests, forbade the people to read or write, skills which they reserved for themselves. This continued until the decline of the Druid cult, when Christian monks began to write down both true stories of Ireland's heroes and heroines, and the myths of folklore and legends. Even before the arrival of Christianity in Ireland, the Celtic Druids had developed a written language, which they carved in stone, often taking up to 12 years to learn the skills. The Celtic alphabet had just 25 letters made up of straight lines, and is known as the Ogham alphabet. Today's Irish language, Gaelic, derives much from the ancient Celtic language.

The main Celtic stories were in three so-called Ulster Cycles. The first told of battles between the supernatural forces which first invaded Ireland. The second is centred around the exploits of the hero Cu Chuliann, a warrior-king with mythical powers, and the third is the Fenian, or Ossianic Cycle.

> *The pleasures of the table are, of all times and all ages, of every country and of every day.'*
>
> *Brillat-Savarin (1755-1826)*

Right: a Janus Stone in Co. Fermanagh.

The Ossianic saga relates the tale of the Fianna, or Fenians, a warrior band under the hero Finn MacColl and his son, Ossian, or Oisin. Many of these tales involved fabled bulls, not just symbols of power and strength, but because cattle formed an integral part of the daily lives of the Celts. The first of the four great Celtic feast days, Sanhain Eve, or Hallowe'en, on November 1st, heralded the end of the grazing season, and the beginning of the Celtic New Year. Fires were extinguished and re-lit, and the fertility of cattle and crops were ensured by the sacrifice of firstborn children. The Celtic summer officially starts on May Day and was named Beltaine, after the fire god, Belenos. The day before Beltaine, cattle would be driven between two fires, in the belief that the smoke from each fire would purge them before they were taken out to pasture. When a new Celtic king had to be selected, the Druids would perform a ritual known as the Tarbhfheis, or bull feast. The Druids would have a bull slaughtered, and then consume its flesh and drink its blood. Sated, they would fall asleep after the feast. During their slumbers they were supposed to dream the new king's name. Many kings and warriors were also buried in bull's hides.

During the Iron Age, farmers fearing cattle rustlers on the shores of Lough Gara, Roscommon, built artificial islands, or crannogs, in the lake. Around 300 of these islands exist, and dugout canoes were used to ferry the cattle over to the islets. Crannogs were in use up until the 1600s.

STOUT-BRAISED BEEF

2 pounds of beef steak cut into ten pieces
3 onions, chopped
4 carrots, halved and sliced lengthwise
3 tablespoons of plain flour
3 tablespoons of vegetable oil
1 teaspoon of honey
1 pint of beef stock
1 pint of stout
1 teaspoon of fresh basil, chopped fine
1 teaspoon of salt and freshly ground black pepper, mixed

Method: *Saute onions in oil and set aside, reserving the oil. Season the flour with salt and pepper and roll the beef in it. Brown the meat in the oil, then set aside with the onions in a pan. Add the rest of the flour to the oil left in the pan. Cook for 2 minutes, then stir in the basil and the stout. Bring to the boil, then add the stock and honey. Put meat, onions and carrots in a casserole dish. Pour over the boiling stock mix, and cover the dish. Cook in a moderate oven for around 1½ hours, or until the meat is tender. The gravy should already be thick, but if desired, it can be thickened a little more with cornflour before serving.*

Right: cattle formed an integral part of the daily lives of the Celts.

At the Simpson-Grant Farm in Derenagh, Dungannon, there is not only the home of the ancestors of Ulysses S Grant, president of the USA from 1869-1877, but also a fine example of an ordered, mid-19th century farm. On its ten acres, three fields were used for grazing two cattle, a horse and a goat, while another three were used to grow a cash crop like flax, used in the making of linen, one was set aside for root crops, and one field was reserved for grain, which also provided straw for bedding and thatching. In the house is a rare example of an ash-pit in front of the hearth, used for cooking potatoes in the hot ash. More sites of agricultural interest can be found near Antrim, where the only surviving water-powered spade mill, Patterson's Mill, is located. Founded in 1919, it was used to forge spades in the traditional way. In County Wexford, at Carley's Bridge, there is Ireland's oldest pottery. Founded in 1659, earthenware cooking pots were made from local clay. It took three months to fill the kilns with hand-made pots, and four days to complete the firing.

STEAK & KIDNEY PUDDING

8 ounces of suet pastry

12 ounces of stewing steak, cubed

4 ounces of kidney, trimmed and quartered

1 onion, chopped fine

2 tablespoons of plain flour

3 tablespoons of stout

1 teaspoon of salt and freshly ground black pepper, mixed

Method: *Half fill a large pan with water. Roll out the pastry, setting aside a quarter of it. Line a greased pudding bowl with the larger portion of pastry. Mix the salt and pepper into the flour, then coat the meat and the kidneys with the seasoned flour. Put the meat and kidneys in a basin. Add the onion and the stout, then roll out the remaining pastry. Dampen the edges of the basin with water. Place the pastry lid on the basin, pressing down the edges all round. Cover with a circle of greaseproof paper, tied on with string. Steam the pudding for 4 hours, then serve it while piping hot.*

Fifteen centuries of Christianity and poetry has given rise to Ireland's favoured nickname, the 'Island of Saints and Scholars'. The famous writer G K Chesterton, said about Dublin, "It is a paradise of poets." From the zealous Saint Patrick of the 4th century, and the magnificent 8th-century *Book of Kells*, to the names of Jonathan Swift, Richard Sheridan and George Bernard Shaw, the Irish have earned the country's reputation as the cradle of Celtic conversion to Christianity, and the creche of literary giants. Oliver Goldsmith, Thomas Moore, Bram Stoker and William Butler Yeats join company with James Joyce, Oscar Wilde, Samuel Beckett, Sean O'Casey, and Brendan Behan.

The vast panoply of Irish literary giants could well be tripled by adding those of Irish descent whose forefathers, like those of several US Presidents, emigrated to far-off lands. For every one of Ireland's current population there are fifteen Irish in foreign lands. The old Celtic saying, that 'There are no strangers in Ireland, only friends we have yet to meet', has a poetic truth and a culinary twist, as most friends meet over a drink or a meal. One dish, enjoyed throughout Ireland and often cooked in large amounts for family celebrations and reunions, is made with pig's trotters and known as crubeens.

CRUBEENS

1 pig's trotter per person
1 onion, halved
1 carrot, quartered
6 peppercorns, crushed
1 bay leaf
1 tablespoon of fresh parsley, chopped
1 teaspoon of thyme
1 teaspoon of salt

Method: *Place all the ingredients in a large pan and cover with cold water. Bring to the boil and simmer for 3 hours. Serve hot or cold, with salad.*

Edmund Burke (1730-1797) was born in Dublin and was educated at Trinity College. This is Ireland's leading University and was founded by Queen Elizabeth Î in 1592. However, none of the 40-acre complex's buildings date from before 1700. James Joyce describes the college buildings in his *Portrait of the Artist as a Young Man* as "...set heavily in the city's ignorance like a dull stone in a cumbrous ring." The main treasure in Trinity College's Library is the famous *Book of Kells*, which dates from around AD800. Burke left Ireland to become a member of Parliament in 1765, at the age of 35, and went on to make his name as an orator and philosophical writer.

Thomas Moore (1779-1852) was also born in Dublin and studied at Trinity College. He moved to London, like Burke, then to Bermuda, where he wrote the *Life of Byron*, and *Irish Melodies*, earning the accolade 'Bard of Erin'. Thomas Moore's words first brought the taste of Irish melodies to the outside world, followed by the works of Charles Villiers Stanford (1852-1924), who taught Vaughan Williams and Gustav Holst.

BACON AND CELERY BAKE

10 stalks of celery, without the leaves, and cut in two
4 ounces of streaky bacon
1 carrot, sliced
1 onion, sliced
1 pint of chicken stock
1 bouquet garni
1 teaspoon of salt and freshly ground black pepper, mixed

Method: *Put the bacon in the bottom of a casserole dish. Add the onion and carrots, then the celery. Pour in the stock, then add the bouquet garni, salt and pepper. Bring to the boil, cover, then turn down the heat. simmer gently for 1½ hours. Serve piping hot with crubeens.*

Mutton is the meat of a sheep over fifteen to eighteen months old, younger than that, it is called lamb. Most mutton bought for the home table is between three and four years old.

Mutton is very popular in Irish recipes, and the local mutton has a firm texture and close grain. Salt meadow mutton is favoured, being raised on pastures rich in wild herbs, clover and shamrock. In the 18th century, some lamb recipes were most ambitious, often recommending seafood as an accompaniment. One popular stuffing for mutton and lamb consisted of oysters, crab meat and anchovy. Some early local recipes also suggested that carragheen, the Irish seaweed, went extremely well with mutton.

In colloquial Irish, joints of meat were sometimes known as 'sproals', while small joints went by the name of 'spoileens'. Spoileens was also the term used for travelling commercial kitchens. These were in the form of tents, in which two fires kept heat under large pots of spoileen, a type of boiled mutton stew sold with bread. These spoileen tents would be found in fairgrounds and at any public celebration, and were very popular across Ireland during the mid-19th century. They were also likely to have been a feature of Cork's famous Old English Market, which dates back to the late 18th century.

KERRY KIDNEYS

8 lamb's kidneys, cored, cleaned and halved
1 pound of small sausages, halved
2 onions, sliced
½ pound of button mushrooms, cleaned and
sliced
2 ounces of butter
1 tablespoon of plain flour
1 pint of stock
1 pint of stout
1 tablespoon of tomato puree
1 teaspoon of salt and freshly ground black
pepper, mixed

Method: *Saute the onions in the butter until brown, then add the sausages. Cook for 1 minute then add the kidneys, browning them with the sausages. Turn into casserole, reserving the butter. And add flour to the reserved butter in the pan, stirring it in. Cook gently until brown, then add the stock, stout and tomato puree. Stir, season, and bring to boil, then pour into the casserole. Cover the casserole and cook it in moderate oven for 1½ hours. Add the mushrooms, then replace in a hot oven for 15 minutes.*

The grass-like leaves of the pink-flowering chives (Allium schoenoprasum), are used in the kitchen in the same way as spring onions, as they also belong to the onion family. Chives are used for their delicate onion flavour and colour in soups, salads, omelettes and sauces. They make a fine garnish and decoration for many dishes. As the leaves contain iron, they are thought to be of help in the treatment of stomach and kidney disorders.

BACON & POTATO SUPPER

1 pound of pork sausages
8 thick slices of back bacon
8 potatoes, sliced
4 onions, sliced
3 tablespoons of parsley, chopped
2 pints of vegetable stock
2 teaspoons of chives, chopped small
1 teaspoon of salt and black pepper, mixed

Method: *Boil the sausages and bacon in the vegetable stock for 5 minutes. Add the other ingredients and season with salt and pepper. Bring to the boil and transfer to a casserole dish. Cover, then gently simmer for 1 hour or until the meat is cooked. When the stew has thickened, sprinkle the chives over the top and serve immediately.*

The Irish are avid smokers, quite apart from the classic image of Irish pub-goers with clay pipes in their mouths! In many country cottages a smoked ham or two hangs from the beams. Smoke-houses exist all over Ireland, as smoked fish and meat increases in popularity. The Irish seem to smoke anything that runs, swims or flies, from beef and pork to pheasant and chicken, and from salmon, haddock and eel to trout, cod and herrings. There are more than a dozen smokehouses in Ireland which smoke ham in the traditional way.

HAM, PEA & POTATO SUPPER

6 ounces of smoked ham, diced small
1 pound of potatoes, cooked and diced
4 courgettes, sliced
4 ounces of peas
1 onion, chopped
2 ounces of butter
1 teaspoon of mustard paste
1 teaspoon of thyme
1 tablespoon of fresh parsley, chopped fine
2 tablespoon of cornflour
4 tablespoons of milk
1 teaspoon of freshly ground black pepper
1 pint of ham stock

Method: *Fry the onions lightly for 3 minutes in half of the butter. Transfer to a large pan and add the stock, ham and peas. Bring up to simmering point and add the potatoes. Mix the mustard, cornflour and milk together, making a paste. Add the mustard mix to the soup, then add the thyme. Steam the courgettes for 5 minutes and add to the mixture. Cook over a moderate heat – not boiling – for 8 minutes. Season with the pepper, then add the rest of the butter. When the butter has melted, sprinkle the parsley over the surface. Serve hot with soda bread.*

Right: garnish of chopped parsley decorates Ham, Pea and Potato Supper.

Animals, both mythical and real, figure heavily in Celtic folklore and legends. They are associated with fertility and growth and are often tied in with the spiritual world. Many are animalised gods and goddesses, while some are anthropomorphised into human shape. Naturally, most common are the domestic animals, cattle, chickens, pigs etc. Birds, like the crow, raven, and wren, enter into several tales, as do fish, especially salmon, and deer, boars, and even wolves. Although there are no snakes in Ireland, several stories relate to serpents' activities and one legend tells how a dragon once ravaged Ireland. The dragon is the one animal which could threaten the fertility of the land and the rule of kings. In another story, the quarrelsome swine herders, Friuch and Rucht, turn themselves into dragons to destroy each other's land with the snow that they were magically able to conjure up.

The Juniper's Latin name, Juniperus communis, indicates that it is part of the cypress family. It is the blue-black fruits of this tree that are used. The berries' oil is used in the treatment of gout, rheumatism, liver and kidney complaints, and as a cleanser to the system. The berries flavour gin, and are infused in water to make a medicinal tea. The berries are also used to flavour game and meat dishes, and are added to marinades for pork and lamb dishes. They are usually crushed before use, and are often added to stews. Since the 1700s, ham in Limerick has traditionally been smoked over a fire containing juniper berries and leaves, giving it its distinctive flavour.

'A watched pot never boils.'

Old Irish saying

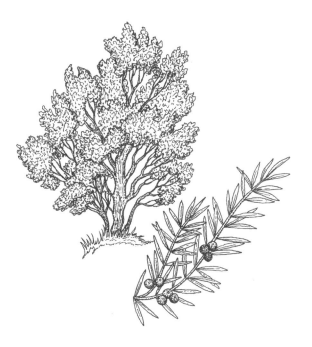

LIMERICK HAM

1 ham on the bone, cured and cooked
1 cup of gin
1 cup of juniper berries
1½ cups of coarse mustard
1 cup of brown sugar

Method: *Deeply score the ham with a knife all over. Rub the juniper berries into the cuts, pushing them in. Mix the gin, sugar and mustard together. Cover the ham all over with the mixture. Place in an ovenproof dish and cover ham with foil. Bake in a hot oven until heated through. Remove foil and bake until the skin is crisp. Baste regularly with the liquid produced.*

Popular, particularly in County Cork, drisheen is the name for a rich, dark, blood sausage, or black pudding. A white variety is unique to County Cork, where it is often served with tripe, and can be made with lamb's blood. Commercially, drisheen is made by combining pig's blood with finely minced pork fat trimmings, onions and herbs. Often oatmeal or breadcrumbs are added, and usually some cream, with herbs like mace, or tansy. This mixture is then poured through a funnel into a long length of pig's gut to form a long coil. The sausage is brushed with blood, which turns black when cooked, and then it is boiled or poached until the blood sets. When drisheen is made in the home, a shallow, wide pan is used in which to steam-bake the sausage in an oven.

Right: oatmeal is an essential ingredient in the Irish version of black pudding, Drisheen

Tansy is a perennial European herb (*Tanacetum vulgare*), and it is often used in cooking as a substitute for nutmeg and cinnamon in desserts, and in soups and stews. Tansy tea is made from an infusion of the leaves, which have a bitter taste, but it is one of the most popular traditional herbal teas.

'Oh! God! that bread should be

so dear,

And flesh and blood so cheap!'

Thomas Hood (1799-1845)

DRISHEEN

2 pints of sheep's blood
2 cups of oatmeal
2 teaspoons of salt
1 pint of full cream milk
1 tablespoon of cream
1 teaspoon of tansy
1 teaspoon of fresh ground black pepper

Method: *Strain the blood into a bowl, then mix in all the ingredients. After leaving it to stand for about an hour, pour the mixture into a greased dish. Place the dish in a large baking dish. Pour water into the larger dish to reach halfway up the smaller dish. Cover the small dish with baking foil. Bake in a medium oven for around 1 hour, or until set. Serve drisheen sliced.*

BACON & CABBAGE SUPPER

10 strips of bacon
1 large Savoy cabbage
5 allspice berries
½ pint of ham stock
½ teaspoon of salt and black pepper, mixed

Method: *Quarter the cabbage, break into leaves, and boil in salted water for 15 minutes. Drain, soak in cold water for 1 minute, drain again and slice. Line an ovenproof dish with five bacon slices. Cover with the cabbage, then sprinkle with allspice and seasoning. Lay the rest of the bacon on top, and pour on the stock. Cover, and simmer for 1 hour until stock is absorbed. Serve hot.*

The legendary Castle of Temperance featured in the 16th-century Irish poet, Edmund Spenser's *Faerie Queene*, had "a stately hall, wherein were many tables fair dispred," was no less than his own residence. In this romance, Spenser describes the castle in great detail, especially the kitchen, with its "goodly parlour with royall arras

richly dight." The castle, now a ruin, stands on Kilcolman Hill in County Cork, and is where the poet and his wife lived from 1580 to 1598. Sir Walter Raleigh visited Spenser in this castle in 1589. Spenser had just been appointed Sheriff of Cork by Queen Elizabeth I, when a revolt broke out. A year before his death in 1599, Spenser and his wife allegedly escaped a deliberate fire – which gutted the castle – by way of an an underground tunnel. It is claimed that one of Spenser's children died in the fire but, in the year 1600, his son, Sylvanus, returned to Kilcolman Castle and refurbished it. Around 300 years later, Ireland's celebrated poet, W B Yeats wrote of the castle, "Could he have gone there as a poet merely, he would have found among wandering storytellers... certainly all the kingdom of Faery, still unfaded, of which his own poetry was often but a troubled image."

In Celtic legend, there was a mythical character named Suibne, who slew St Ronan Finn's acolyte with a spear, then tried to kill the saint himself. Ronan cursed Suibne to fly like the spear and to die by a spear. At the Battle of Magh Rath in AD637, at Moira, in County Down, Suibne was driven mad by the din of the battle. He began perching in the branches of trees, making up poems. Suibne eventually sat in the branches of a tree outside St Mullins' home. The saint ordered his cook to feed Suibne, who daily drank the gift of milk from a hollowed-out cow pat. A neighbour told the cook's husband that she was favouring Suibne over him. The cook's husband then took a spear and killed Suibne, thus fulfilling the curse.

GAMMON WITH WHISKEY SAUCE

4 gammon steaks, trimmed of fat
½ an onion, finely chopped or grated
1 teaspoon of soft brown sugar
2 tablespoons of plain flour
2 tablespoons of butter
1 tablespoon of salted butter
2 teaspoons of Irish whiskey
1 cup of stock
1 teaspoon of salt and ground black pepper, mixed

Method: *Soften the unsalted butter and brush half on one side of the steaks. Grill steaks, buttered side up, for 7 minutes. Turn the steaks, butter their upper sides, and repeat the grilling time. To make the sauce, fry the onions in the salted butter. When golden, remove from heat and stir in the flour. Add stock and return to the heat. Add sugar, then bring to the boil, stirring. Simmer for 2 minutes and add whiskey and seasoning. Serve the gammon with the sauce poured over them.*

CABBAGE & CORNED BEEF

2 pounds of corned beef brisket
Half a head of cabbage (about 1 pound)
3 carrots, peeled and halved
1 onion
4 potatoes, peeled and quartered
1 teaspoon of dried thyme
1 teaspoon of fresh parsley, chopped fine
6 cloves

For the sauce:
½ pint of double cream
3 tablespoons of prepared horseradish
1 tablespoon of mayonnaise

Method: *In a large pan, cover the meat with water and bring it to the boil. Press the cloves into the onion and add it to the pan. Add thyme and parsley, then simmer for 1 hour. Skim the fat from the surface. Add the cabbage, potatoes and carrots. Simmer for around 25 minutes, or until cabbage is cooked. Take off heat, remove the meat and cut it into small pieces. Strain the vegetables and serve them with the meat.*
For the sauce: Whip the cream until it is stiff. Fold in the mayonnaise and horseradish. Serve with the corned beef and cabbage.

Right: *it was in the 11th century that the pipes were first recorded as an accompaniment to Irish dancing.*

Ireland is synonymous with music. It is also the only country which has a musical instrument as its national symbol, the harp. It was in the 11th century that the pipes were first recorded as an accompaniment to Irish dancing, and harp music was the traditional background to the music of Carolan (1670-1738), who wrote more than 200 tunes. The line-up of traditional musical instruments also includes the ancient bodhran, or small hand-held goatskin drum. The elbow pipes, or uilleann, had replaced the mouth-blown pipes by the 18th century, and were joined by the violin, or fiddle, in the late 1700s. A famous 18th-century Irish fiddler is celebrated in Ballek, during the Fiddle Stone Festival. In 1792, a huge harp festival was held in Belfast, introducing Edward Bunting's collection of traditional Irish tunes.

The promotion of traditional Irish music and culture, celebrated in festivals known as 'Fleadh', is looked after by the Comhaltas Ceoltoiri Eireann. Apart from the promotion of Gaelic music, Irish culture and folklore is celebrated and jealously preserved by the Irish Folklore Commission. One famous Fleadh is held in August, in Enniscorthy, County Wexford, although every town and county holds some musical celebration or fair.

Feakle, in County Clare, for example, hosts the International Traditional Music Festival each August. Also held in the same month, the Puck Fair, in Killorglin, County Kerry, is one of the oldest traditional Irish festivals. Another festival of traditional music, song and dance, is Ballycastle's Fleadh Amhran agus Rince. The Antrim Glens host the Feis na n Gleann, celebrating the 19th-century interest in Irish culture and sport. There is also the Carolan Harp Festival in Keadue, County Roscommon, and the Siamsa Tire, which is the Gaelic name for Ireland's National Theatre, which is based in Tralee.

The Gaelic word for hostels is 'bruiden', an ancient word for hospitality centres that were once dotted across Ireland. These forerunners of the modern public house were more than just drinking and sleeping lodges. They were originally religious centres for the Druids, who offered open house to travellers. A great cauldron was kept boiling in the centre of all the bruidens, which were often the scene of great feasts and celebrations. The surviving descriptions of early bruidens suggest that they were built over, or on both sides of sacred streams, and were said to glow with a fierce firelight.

This compounds the theme, found running through mythological history, referring to the magical combination of fire and water. This magic is said to have first confounded the attackers of the Bruiden da Derga, before they destroyed it. The Derga bruiden was located in Glencree in County Wicklow, not far from Coolakay House, which today has an agricultural centre and a museum with depictions of farm life over the centuries.

COLD HONEY-GLAZED HAM

1 smoked ham
1 large onion
3 tablespoons of honey
8 cloves
6 peppercorns, crushed
2 tablespoons of vinegar
2 tablespoons of soft brown sugar

Method: *Soak the ham in water overnight. Drain, then put ham in a pan, covered with fresh water. Stud the onion with cloves. Add the onion, peppercorns and half of the honey to the pan containing the ham. Bring it to the boil. Skim off the scum and simmer for around 20 minutes. Remove ham from pan and peel off the ham's skin. Replace the skinless ham in the stock and allow it to cool. Heat the brown sugar, vinegar and the rest of the honey, stirring until mixed. When the ham has cooled, drain off the stock. Pour the honey mixture over the ham and let it cool. Serve it thinly sliced.*

Some of Ireland's wondrous myths and ballads are comparatively recent, and some relate to local recreations, like its celebrated horse racing and the ancient Irish sport of hurling, a game invented by the early Celts. The All Ireland Hurling Final is held every September at Croke Park, Dublin.

Almost every Irish town or village has its fairy tale, and many places have their own fairy thorn bush, or 'sceach'. Originally, the word 'faierie' meant a state of entrancement, but in the 17th century it became the word for supernatural creatures between men and angels – such as dwarves, elves, merpeople etc. The legendary fairy war between the 'little people' of Kerry and Connacht is locally believed to continue, and Kilrea in County Derry holds an annual Fairy Thorn Festival.

The celebrated 250-year-old Kilrae thorn is said to be home to the local fairies, and in some areas the fairy glen is often a hazel copse. Hazel is legendary in Ireland for its magical powers, and figures in several local folklores. It is also said that a miniature fairy book was found in the grounds of Gilford Castle, County Armagh, which gave instructions on how to wake the local fairies from their 700-year sleep. The Queen's University in Belfast even offers a degree course in fairy studies.

"The provisions of this city (Dublin) are, in general, exceeding good, and at a reasonable price, more especially liquors. The best spirits may be had at half the price they sell for in London. But it is remarkable that, notwithstanding the general conveniences here, they are defective of proper accommodation for travellers, there not being a place of public entertainment in the city, that deserves the name of an inn."

From 'A New Royal Authentic and Complete System of Universal Geography', Printed in 1790.

Chapter Seven

COCKLES, MUSSELS, PRAWNS & LOBSTERS

'Mussels are the food of kings,

limpets are the food of peasants.'

Old Irish saying

Every Irishman knows the tales of Cu Chulainn, hero of many a local legend, Irish warrior lord, and the nephew of King Conchobar. At five years old, he began to demonstrate his superhuman powers, and later fell in love with Emer, the daughter of one of his opponents. Furthering the Greek elements in Irish legend, Emer's father sent Cu Chulainn to fight the Amazon female warrior, Scathach, in the hope that he would be killed. Instead, the Amazon taught him to use the sun-god's spear, the 'Gae Bolga'.

At that time, Bricriu was Ulster's lord. He had built a new palace and had invited Cu Chulainn, Conall and Loeghaire, the three barons of Ulster, to feast with him. Bricriu offered them a Potion of Champions, after a challenge, promising that the winner of the tournament would be the one whose wife was the first wife to enter the chieftain's hall. Chulainn made a chink in the wall to let his wife through first, but Bricriu had another test in mind for the three contestants.

In one version of this traditional tale, the barons were sent to fight a mythical magic monster, but only Chulainn took up the challenge. After the fight, a giant appeared, flourishing an axe that was said to be able to 'part a hair aloft in the wind'. The giant invited any of the three to cut off his

head – provided that he could cut off theirs the next day! Propitiously, Conall and Loeghaire declined the offer. Relying on his supernatural powers, Chulainn sliced off the giant's head. The following morning, the giant returned from the dead to exact his revenge, according to the pact. However, instead of bringing the blade of his axe down on Chulainn's neck, the giant reversed his axe, hitting Chulainn with the blunt back of the axe. Cu Chulainn was immediately proclaimed champion of Ulster, and went on to protect Ireland from waves of invaders. Cu Chulainn was finally killed by Lugaid, the son of one of his victims.

Right; a selection of seafood; all to be found around the Irish coastlines.

In 1734, a woman known as Molly Malone was buried in St John's Churchyard, south-east of Dublin, at Blackrock. This is said to be the Molly of the famous rhyme, who wheeled her wheelbarrow through Dublin's broad and narrow streets, '...selling cockles and mussels, alive, alive-o!' At the bottom of Grafton Street in Dublin, there is a voluptuous statue of Molly, together with her well-stocked barrow.

In the second century – well before Molly Malone's peregrinations – communities of fisherfolk lived on the wild, western coast of Ireland. Typical is Omey Island, on the most western tip of County Galway. St Fechin established this small community in the year AD700. He left behind him the ruins of his church, the Teampull Fechin, and a well of spring water called Tobair Fechin, or Fechin's Well. Here, in the rushy bogs, is evidence of the community's past existence in the ruins of small dwellings, half sunk into the ancient earth. Behind these dwellings are 'middens', large mounds of refuse from the local kitchens. From these middens, the diet of these Irish ancestors can be determined. Predominant amongst the refuse are millions of shells of limpets and cockles, with the occasional bones from bear, deer, and wild boar.

Right: the voluptuous statue of Molly Malone.

ONION MUSSELS

30 mussels, cleaned and sorted
6 large onions, sliced
4 shallots, chopped
5 garlic cloves
1 carrot, chopped
2 sticks of celery, chopped
3 potatoes, sliced
6 chicory leaves, chopped
1 sprig of thyme and a bay leaf, tied together
1 tablespoon of fresh parsley, chopped fine
1 ounce of butter
4 fluid ounces of water
4 fluid ounces of white wine
1 teaspoon of freshly ground black pepper

Method: *On a high heat, cook mussels in wine and water until they open. Discard those that remain closed, and strain off liquor. Saute onions in butter in a pan, add shallots and garlic. Add potatoes, celery, chicory and carrots. Add tied herbs and the mussel liquor, then add pepper. Simmer for 1 hour, then add mussels and serve after 2 minutes.*

'A ferthyng-worth of muscles

were a

feste for suche folke.'

From 'Piers Plowman's Creed', Langland 1393

Ireland's coastal waters provide ideal conditions in which clams thrive. To the west of Ireland are the deeps of the Atlantic Ocean, while to the east are the shallower waters of the Irish Sea. There are around ten types of native clam which are to be found in the seas around Ireland. Most are quite small but the popular, large Hardshell clam has been introduced from its native North America into the waters around the south coast of Ireland.

In Northern Ireland the name for the Soft-shelled clam, which is the largest of the local species found in Ireland, is 'Brallion'. There are still many cocklers around Ireland's sandy coasts, raking the flats for the sought-after clams and cockles. The local fishers around Derrynane harbour, County Kerry, also have an odd method of ensnaring the delicious razorfish, which bury themselves in the soft sand when the tide goes out. Razorfish, a shellfish, have long, thin, sharp shells. Usually – but not always – they have to be dug out of the sand with a pronged rake.

In Derrynane, the locals sprinkle salt on the sand, where small holes reveal the presence of razorfish. The acrid intensity of the increased salt content causes the shellfish to propel themselves out of their lairs, allowing them to be caught as they leap into the air!

COCKLE SOUP

4 dozen cockles, cleaned and cooked with their broth
2 tablespoons of plain flour
2 ounces of butter
2 celery stalks, chopped
2 fluid ounces of double cream
1 pint of milk
1 teaspoon of salt
1 teaspoon of ground black pepper
Juice of 1 lemon
1 tablespoon of parsley, chopped fine

Method: *Separate the cockle meat and broth from their shells. Make a roux with the melted butter and flour, stirring for 1 minute. Strain the cockle broth into the mixture gradually, stirring all the time until it is smooth. Add celery, parsley, salt, pepper and lemon juice. Cook over a low heat, stirring for 8 minutes. Add the cockles, and cook for 3 more minutes. Serve the soup with a swirl of cream on top.*

Right: County Kerry; these Irish coastal waters provide ideal conditions in which clams thrive.

Mussels are usually sold by weight, or by the measure, and the people of County Kildare swear by their mussels which come from Bannow Bay. When preparing mussels, they should be soaked in cold water for about an hour, during which time any that float should be discarded, as should any broken mussels and those which do not close when tapped sharply. The shells should be scrubbed clean, barnacles and weed removed, and then de-bearded with a knife.

Both mussels and cockles can be eaten raw or prepared, as in the days of yore, when they were cooked on a heated stone. Before eating or cooking shellfish, they should be left in a container of sea, or salt water to purge. As mussels contain a little toxin, a pinch of bicarbonate of soda in the cooking water will neutralise it. Care should be taken not to overcook mussels. Some of the best mussels in the whole of Ireland are found on the wild coasts of the west of the island. These are now commercial packaged and exported around the globe. Murphy's International Mussel Fair is held every May in Bantry, County Cork. Although mussels are generally regarded as a poor man's food, they are highly regarded in France, especially in the north-west, an area which has long links with Ireland. This is well demonstrated at the French Festival, held in July, which celebrates the links between DunLaoghaire and Brest, a town in France.

BRALLION CLAM CHOWDER

2 dozen Irish Brallion clams, washed
4 potatoes, diced small
1 ounce of butter
5 teaspoons of chives, chopped fine
2 tablespoons of plain flour
1 pint of milk
1 tablespoon of milk

Method: *Put clams in a pan and cover with water. Cover the pan. Boil the clams until they open. Discard any which do not open. Take the clams from the shells, clean, and remove beards. Keep the clam water, and cut the clams into pieces. Put the clams back into the water with the pint of milk and the potatoes. Stir in the butter and cook, simmering for 30 minutes. Add the chives and simmer for a further 15 minutes. Mix the flour into a paste with the tablespoon of milk. Stir in the paste to thicken the soup. Serve when bubbling hot.*

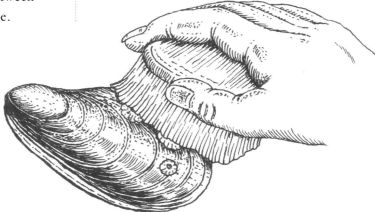

'Soft words butter no turnips, but neither will they harden the heart of a cabbage.'

Old Irish saying

DUBLIN BAY PRAWNS IN ASPIC

6 Dublin Bay prawns, peeled and prepared
1 large handful of carragheen
1 bay leaf
2 cloves
2 sprigs of parsley
Pinch of salt
1 teaspoon of vinegar
Two lemon slices

Method: *Soak carragheen in water for 15 minutes, then drain it. Put the carragheen, 1 parsley sprig, bay leaf, cloves, and salt in a pan. Simmer carragheen, in 1 pint of water for 1 hour. Stir in one teaspoon of vinegar. Place prawns in a bowl, or mould, and strain the carragheen liquor over the prawns. Chill and let set. Turn out onto a plate and garnish with parsley and lemon slices.*

Also known as the Norway lobster, the reddish-orange Dublin Bay prawn, or pink prawn, has a body around 8 inches (20cm) in length, with long, narrow, striped claws. Dublin Bay prawns do not change colour when cooked, unlike many other crustaceans. This marine crustacean, the source of scampi, does not come from Dublin Bay, but is found in Atlantic waters. The name comes from the fact that the Dublin fishing fleet once sailed into port with a quantity of these prawns mixed in with their catch. The fishermen would then distribute the prawns to itinerant street-vendors, as they had no value in the fish markets. So the prawns' name came from the bay where the street-vendors got their wares.

Once known as Succory, Chicory (Cichorium intybus), can grow as tall as a man. The leaves and roots have a bitter quality. Chicory is used in salads and as a vegetable, and also in some medicinal preparations. Ground, dried chicory can be used as an additive to coffee, or sometimes even as a substitute for coffee. Chicory adds almost a piquant flavour to the following traditional recipe.

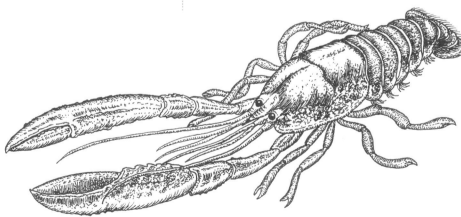

TRADITIONAL DUBLIN BAY PRAWN COCKTAIL

10 Dublin Bay prawn tails, cooked and prepared
2 sprigs of parsley, chopped
8 medium-sized lettuce leaves
8 chicory leaves
8 lemon slices
2 teaspoons of malt vinegar
2 teaspoons of fresh grated horseradish
1 teaspoon of tomato puree
1 teaspoon of Worcestershire sauce
3 drops of Tabasco sauce
4 tablespoons of whipped cream
Pinch of salt
Pinch of freshly ground black pepper

Method: *Mix the last 8 ingredients together to make the sauce, or use one from the 'Classic Sauces' chapter. Chop the prawns into cubes. Mix the prawns into the sauce. Line four bowls with the lettuce and chicory leaves. Spoon the prawn mixture into the bowls. Garnish with the parsley and lemon slices.*

The shrimp found in the waters around Ireland are the Brown Shrimp variety, and are generally less than half the size of the smallest prawns. However, as with the prawns, shrimp are now highly valued in Ireland. To prepare fresh shrimp for the chowder dish, they should be boiled quickly for a few minutes, during which time they will turn from brown to pink. When cool, the heads should be pinched off, and the leg parts pinched out, when the shell will come away from the body and tail. When thus prepared, shrimps in Ireland are often traditionally potted in butter, together with a pinch of nutmeg and a drop or two of anchovy essence.

IRISH SHRIMP CHOWDER

1 pint of shrimps, shelled
2 ounces of hard Irish cheese, grated
3 medium-sized potatoes, sliced
1 ounce of butter
1 large onion, sliced
1 pint of milk
1 tablespoon of fresh parsley, chopped fine
1 teaspoon of salt and freshly ground black pepper, mixed
1 pint of boiling water

Method: *Saute the onion in the butter until translucent. Add the water, potatoes, salt and pepper. Cover and simmer for 15 minutes. When potatoes are tender, add the shelled shrimps and milk. Bring to the boil and stir in the cheese and parsley. Reduce heat and simmer for 5 minutes. Serve while hot.*

When preparing lobsters after boiling, let the lobster cool, rub it with oil and place on its back on a board. Where the lobster's last pair of legs joins the body, insert a sharp knife and bisect the tail. Similarly, bisect the body section. Remove the dark thread and sac near the head, which is the gut and stomach, from body and tail, and the gritty part at the top of the head. The lobster can now be removed from its shell, or cooked on a barbecue in its two half shells. The green part, the lobster's liver, and the creamy part, together with the coral-coloured part – the roe of the hen, or female lobster – can be reserved for mixing with a sauce. The larger parts of the lobster's two claws contain a white meat which can also be removed with the aid of a hammer and a skewer. This dish can be quite expensive, and is sometimes known as Dublin Lawyer, for reasons the reader can easily work out!

Right: Dublin Bay prawns, also known as Norway lobsters.

POTTED IRISH CRAB

Meat from a 2-pound boiled crab
8 ounces of unsalted butter
1 ounce of clarified butter
½ teaspoon of allspice
½ teaspoon of Cayenne pepper
½ teaspoon of salt and freshly ground black
pepper, mixed
1 teaspoon of lemon juice

Method: *Separate the firm crab meat from the creamy meat. Season both firm and creamy meat with allspice and Cayenne. Mix in the pepper, salt, and lemon juice to both meats. Spoon the meat mixture in layers of each type of meat, into ramekins. Melt the butter and pour it slowly over meat in ramekins. Let the butter soak into the meat. Place ramekins in a pan of water. Bake for 25 minutes in a moderate oven. Let cool, then pour clarified butter over each ramekin to seal the top.*

DUBLIN LAWYER

1 fresh lobster, around 2½ pounds in weight,
cleaned as described on page 102
6 tablespoons of garlic butter
8 ounces of single cream (double cream for a
lawyer!)
4 tablespoons of Irish whiskey
½ teaspoon of salt and freshly ground black
pepper, mixed

Method: *In a heavy pan, warm the butter until frothing. Cut lobster into chunks and mix with the coral meat. Take all the lobster meat and cook lightly in the butter for about four minutes. Warm the whiskey, and flame it over lobster. When flames die down, pour in the cream. Heat, but do not boil, for a few minutes. Place the meat back into the halved shells and pour over sauce. Season with salt and pepper and serve hot.*

To prepare a crab, after boiling and letting it cool, first lay it on its back on a board, having twisted off the claws and legs. Putting the pressure of two thumbs behind and under the body of the crab, between its top shell and hard tail parts, lever the body from the shell. Remove the stomach bag, or sac, which lies in the top of the shell, and any green or spongy substance left in the shell. Scoop out the meat remaining in the shell, and retain. Discard the remaining skin-like caul, the gills, and the greyish pieces often called 'dead man's fingers', from the body. Press on the small mouth part of the crab's body, and this should snap away. Scoop out the meat from the claws and legs by cracking them. Add this to the meat from the shell. The white meat can be kept separate from the brown-coloured meat, which is found in the sides of the shell. To remove white meat from what is left of the body, cut the body in two and extract the meat with a skewer, taking care not to include the brittle shell pieces.

'....scorn not garlic like some

that think

it only maketh man winke and

drinke and stinke.'

Sir John Harrington, 1609

Right: cooked crabs ready for preparation.

To serve crab in its shell, wash shell thoroughly then take a cloth, breaking the bottom parts of the shell away, where it is clearly defined, leaving a small rim around the underside of the main shell. The meat can then be placed in the shells in stripes of brown and white meat.

Some cooks also add stripes of chopped, boiled whites of egg, and the brown meat mashed together with pepper, salt, mustard, and the cooked yolks. Finely chopped parsley is generally used to garnish a dressed crab.

Chapter Eight

TROSC & CODLING

Linked inextricably to the sea or its many rivers and lakes, the people of Ireland live on an island surrounded by waters prolific in fish and seafood. Many of the Celtic legends are based around sea voyages, not the least of which was that of Bran, or Bendigeid Vran, son of Llyr. He invaded Ireland to rescue his sister, but was a celebrated voyager and later went to look for the Other World with 27 friends. On his return to Ireland, nobody recognised him, and so he was left to wander for the rest of his life. However, seven of his followers traced him to England, where they cut off his head, burying it on the current site of the Tower of London.

One of Ireland's most extraordinary legends, related along the north and west coasts from Antrim to Kerry, is that of the mermaid. It is said that a fisherman once found the cloak of a mermaid left on the rocky shoreline. He took the cloak home and concealed it in a hidden cupboard. The fisherman was followed by the mermaid, who became his wife. The couple had several children but, one day, the mermaid discovered her cloak and immediately returned to the sea. Even today, some coastal families believe that they are descended from the fisherman and his mermaid wife. They also relate the tale of how the plaice got its crooked mouth.

Parsley (Petroselinum crispium), is an effective antidote to the smell of garlic, and it also reduces uric acid. It contains amounts of vitamin A, carotene, potassium, calcium and iron. Parsley is more commonly used as a culinary decoration, but it does have a distinct flavour of its own, which comes out in parsley sauce, usually used with fish. Parsley tea is a good source of iron, occasionally drunk as a tonic and as a remedy for rheumatism. Every monastery had its own fishpond, usually stocked with carp or trout, to provide the traditional Friday meal. An early herbalist monk once declared that, if sprigs of parsley were thrown into the monastery's fishpond, it would "heal the sick fishes therein." In the following recipe for irish Trosc Bake, commonly served for supper, parsley is just used as a garnish for the trosc, which is the Irish word for cod.

Right: the cliffs of Moher in County Clare.

IRISH TROSC BAKE

1 pound of fresh cod fillet, skinned and cubed
1 pound of potatoes, sliced thin
1 onion, grated
2 ounces of mushrooms, sliced
10 ounces of ready-made tomato soup
1 tablespoon of fresh parsley, chopped fine
1 teaspoon of salt and freshly ground black
pepper, mixed

Method: *Cook potatoes in boiling, salted water for 10 minutes, then drain. Lay the fish cubes in a greased baking dish. Top with onion, mushrooms, and a layer of potato slices. Season with salt and pepper. Pour the tomato soup over the potatoes. Bake in a hot oven for around 25 minutes. Serve when the tomato soup bubbles, garnished with the chopped parsley.*

Codling is the name given to small cod, a round fish which is common in Irish waters, and one of the most popular fish for its versatility. Cod – known as Trosc in Ireland – and codling, can be cooked in just about any way, baked, fried, grilled, poached, or steamed. A cod can range in weight from just over a pound, to 20 pounds, and is often cut into steaks, or cutlets, when it is large. Cod is at its best from May until October, and the Irish Fishery Authorities have described the cod's colouring as similar to that of Connemara marble: sandy overall, but with flecks and mottlings of green and brown. Both cod and codling can be dried and salted, when it should be soaked in cold water overnight to revive its consistency.

COCKLED CODLING

1 pound of codling fillets, cleaned
2 dozen cockles, cleaned
6 potatoes, halved and cooked
3 small onions, sliced
1 ounce of butter, melted
1 teaspoon of fresh thyme, chopped fine
1 tablespoon of fresh parsley, chopped fine
1 tablespoon of fennel, chopped fine
1 half lemon, sliced
1 teaspoon of salt and black pepper, mixed

Method: *Parboil the onion slices and set aside. Place fish in a baking dish, season with salt, pepper and thyme. Boil the cockles, covered in water, until they open. Discard any that do not open. Remove the cockles from their shells and clean, keeping hot. Pour the juice from the cockle pan over the fish. Place onions and potatoes around the fish, add melted butter. Bake in a hot oven, basting occasionally, for 15 minutes.*

The Monkfish has a large, broad head and gaping mouth, with two large fins on either side of its tapering body. In Medieval times, because the fins reminded fishermen of wings, they named it the Angel fish. In the late 1500s, Rondelet describes the head of the fish as being likened to a man's face, and the fins like arms, or the cloak of a monk. Its present name, monkfish, probably stems from his observations. Because this tasty fish looks rather unattractive, it is rarely seen on the fishmonger's slab, and today its fine meat is used in processing snacks like seafood sticks, or mock scampi.

CODDLED MONKFISH

2 Monkfish fillets, around ½ pound each, cleaned
1 onion, sliced
6 potatoes, cooked and mashed with 1 ounce of butter
1 ounce of butter
1 cup of milk
1 yolk, and white of egg, separated
4 sprigs of fresh parsley
2 lemons, cut into wedges

For the paste:
3 tablespoons of brown breadcrumbs
1 ounce of butter, melted
2 teaspoons of lemon juice
1 tablespoon of fresh parsley, chopped fine
1 teaspoon of dried tarragon and dill, mixed
Pinch of salt and pepper

Method: *Combine the sauce ingredients into a paste. Place one fillet in the bottom of a greased baking dish. Smear the paste over the fillet and place the other fillet on top of it. Pour the milk around the fish and arrange the onion slices on top. Cover the fish with foil and bake in a moderate oven for 30 minutes. Mix the egg yolk into mashed potato. Beat the egg white until stiff, then fold it into the potato. Remove the fish from the oven and cover it with the mashed potato mix. Bake for 15 minutes until the top is lightly browned.*

In the *Seanchus Mor*, dated AD441, it was recorded that the growing of barley was reserved solely for brewing purposes. However, during the 7th century, there is also a reference to a honey beer, or mead, in the life of Saint Berach in Ireland. On excavating the remains of part of 10th-century Dublin, remains were found which revealed that Ireland's Viking community not only dined on strawberries, plums and cherries, as well as grapes and figs, but also enjoyed apples. It is therefore quite probable that they brewed a form of cider. It was known that, at least until the 9th century, hops were not used in brewing in the north of Ireland, where a beer was made from honey and flowers of the heathland, such as broom, wormwood, and other herbs. Mead was a popular beverage in Ireland well up to the 12th century, and it is recorded in the 1107 *Annals of Ulster* that the drink was known as 'miodh', or 'mil-fion', an alcoholic mixture of fermented honey and water called 'honey-wine'. Today, as well as brewing Ireland's famous stout, Irish cider is also made and has grown in popularity.

An old Irish remedy for toothache goes back to the loaves and fishes of biblical times. It is said that to carry two haddock jawbones in your pocket, is a potent preventative against toothache. The older the bones are, the more powerful the magic.

Haddock in Cider

6 fillets of haddock, boned and skinned
½ pound of mushrooms
½ pint of dry cider
2 ounces of butter
1 tablespoon of plain flour
1 tablespoon of milk
2 teaspoons of fresh dill, chopped
1 teaspoon of salt and black pepper, mixed

Method: *Lay fillets in a greased baking dish and cover with cider. Season, then cover the dish, bringing the cider up to simmering point. Poach fish for about 10 minutes. Fry the mushrooms in half the butter and set aside, keeping warm. Add the rest of butter to the pan. When melted, stir in the flour to make a roux. Cook for 1 minute, then gradually add the milk and a little fish juice. Stir together to make a sauce, then mix in the dill. Arrange the mushrooms over the fish and pour on the sauce. Brown under the grill and serve hot.*

In Gaelic, the name for flounders is 'fluke', and they are commonly only caught in the shallows and rockpools of western Ireland. County Mayo is the location of a famous rockpool, or ocean blowhole, named the 'Poll na Seantine', or Hole of the Ancient Fire. Legend has it that the evil Crom Dubh inhabited a fort on the cliffs here. He tried to burn Saint Patrick with a wind of flames, but the saint drove the flaming wind through the rocks and into the sea, thus creating the blowhole. Saint Patrick then destroyed Crom Dubh and his fort with one blow from his staff, slicing off that part of the cliff and forming the nearby Stack of Dun Brute, a 200-foot high stone pillar. One of the best-known legends about Saint Patrick is that of the Children of Lir, whose jealous mother turned them into swans. Nine hundred years later, when the swans swam past St Patrick on Inishglora Island, he turned them back into human form, when they came ashore and died, thus receiving a Christian burial.

Tarragon Fluke

2 fillets of flounder, cleaned
3 ounces of butter
1 tablespoon of plain flour
1 clove of garlic, crushed
2 tablespoons of tarragon leaves, chopped fine
1 teaspoon of vegetable oil
2 tablespoons of lemon juice
½ teaspoon of salt and black pepper, mixed

Method: *Mix together half the tarragon, lemon juice and garlic. Marinade the fish in the mixture for 30 minutes. Heat half of the butter in a pan until the foam subsides. Season the flour and coat the fish fillets. Turn the fish in the hot butter until coated. Cook fish, without turning, for around 5 minutes, until white. Mix the remaining tarragon with the butter and oil. Form into two butter pats, and serve on the cooked fish.*

Right: an Irish fish monger displays a variety of produce available from the coastal waters of Ireland.

This is an old Irish recipe for haddock, or 'cadog', in mornay, or cheese sauce, with local scones. At one time, the haddock caught in Dublin Bay were as famous and sought-after as its prawns. Salting tends to ruin the delicate flavour of haddock, so the Irish preserved them by drying and smoking. In some places, haddock was traditionally dried in the sun.

CADOG COBBLER

1½ pounds of skinless haddock, boned and cleaned
8 ounces of plain flour
2 ounces of butter
1 teaspoon of baking powder
3 ounces of medium cheese, grated
1 egg yolk
3 tablespoons of milk
Pinch of salt

For the sauce:
1 pint of Bechamel sauce
6 ounces of hard cheese, grated fine
1 teaspoon of mustard powder
2 teaspoons of milk

Method: *Mix the mustard to a paste with the milk. Heat the Bechamel sauce to below boiling. Stir in the mustard mix. Stir the cheese into the sauce and heat gently. Set aside. Cut the fish into pieces and place in a greased dish. Pour the cheese sauce over the fish. Make scones by combining the flour, butter, baking powder and salt. Mix in half of the grated cheese and the egg yolk. Make the mixture into a dough by mixing in the milk. Roll the dough out, then cut it into small, thick scones. Place scones over the fish and dot the scones' tops with milk. Sprinkle the rest of the grated cheese over each scone. Bake in a hot oven for around 30 minutes, until scones brown.*

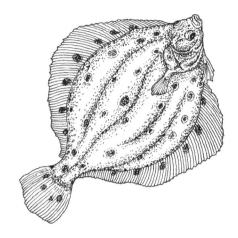

> *"Fresh ling we'll have and*
>
> *mackerel,*
>
> *with lobster, crab and wrasse;*
>
> *The turbot too will be there,*
>
> *the gurnet and the bass.*
>
> *And noble though the pike is,*
>
> *arrayed upon a dish,*
>
> *In splendour none can rival*
>
> *the salmon, prince of fish."*
>
> Anthony Raftery (1784-1835), the 'Blind Bard of the West'

'Leathog', is Irish for plaice, and there are Gaelic names for most common sea fish. It may be useful to have some of these names to hand when eating fish in the more remote, country parts of Ireland, although the pronunciation may be difficult. The brill fish is known in Irish as 'broit', the gurnard is called 'crudan', and wrasse are known as 'ballach', conger eel and the common eel are called 'eascu', and common ling is 'longa'. In Gaelic, the whiting is 'faoitin' and, in Northern Ireland, the scad is known as 'crake herring'.

STUFFED LEATHOG

Two fillets of plaice, around ½ pound each, cleaned
1 cup of milk
6 potatoes, cooked and mashed
1 onion, sliced
1 ounce of margarine
Yolk and white of egg, separate

For the sauce:
3 tablespoons of soft breadcrumbs
1 ounce of butter
1 teaspoon of mixed herbs
½ teaspoon of freshly ground black pepper

Method: *Place the bottom fish fillet in a greased dish, skin side down. Mix together the stuffing ingredients, and spread this on the fillet. Place the top fillet, flesh side down, on the stuffing. Pour in the milk, then scatter in the onion slices. Cover with greaseproof paper and cook in a hot oven for 30 minutes. Mash the margarine and egg yolk into the potatoes. Fold in the white of egg, and cover the fish with the potato mixture. Brown in the oven for around 15 minutes. Remove from the oven, and serve with parsley sauce*

IRISH SEAWEEDS

Carragheen, named after the Irish village, is commonly known as Irish moss. However, it is not a moss but a fan-like, purple-red, marine plant resembling moss. There are two varieties of this seaweed, the other one being commonly known as Stackhouse. Carragheen, sometimes spelt without the 'h', contains the gelatinous agar-agar, or isinglass. This is a thickening agent used by vegetarians as a substitute for gelatine. This seaweed will keep for years if dried and bleached, and is used in a variety of Irish savoury and dessert dishes. In Northern Ireland, this seaweed is also mixed into hot milk, as a pudding or a nightcap. The reddish-purple, or reddish-green plant is used in clarifying beer, in ice-cream, and in cosmetics and medicines. The plant is said to ease indigestion and aid sleep. Carragheen is good for thickening fish stews and soups, and is usually bought dried, but has to be washed and cleaned of grit before cooking. In County Donegal and on the shores of Ulster, another form of edible seaweed is found, which has the highest iron content of any food, and is said to prevent seasickness. This is known locally as dulce, or 'dilisk' (Palmaria palmata), deriving its Latin name from its frond-like shape.

Right: the seaweed covered coastline of Ireland.

Sloke

Also known as 'laver' in Wales, where the jelly-like substance called 'laverbread' is made from this reddish seaweed, sloke, or 'slugane' (Porphyra umbilicalis), has long been revered in the Irish kitchen. In a museum in Dublin, there is evidence of the reverence that even the Irish aristocracy had for sloke, as one Georgian exhibit is a beautiful silver sloke pot with a long wooden handle.

One variety of this edible seaweed is called by its Latin name, Porphyra purpurae, which means 'purple giant'. When cooked, this red-tinged seaweed turns a greenish colour. It is often used as a local coastal vegetable, or can be added fresh to salads. There are several ways to cook sloke, which is generally bought already boiled from the shops and markets. It is usually boiled for several hours, when it turns out as a dark-green mush. After buying, sloke is commonly cooked again in milk, then pressed to remove as much moisture as possible, producing a texture akin to that of well-cooked spinach. After this, it is chopped finely, mixed, or coated with oatmeal, and fried, together with bacon or in bacon fat, until it is golden brown on both sides. Sloke is said to be a good cure for indigestion, coughs and colds, and it is rich in iodine, calcium, potassium, sodium, iron and the vitamins B and C.

Sea Kale

Although not a seaweed, Sea Kale is another coastal vegetable cultivated and used in traditional Irish cookery. Because this salt-resistant, cabbage-like vegetable turns brown and bitter when exposed to sunlight during growing, sea kale is 'earthed up', much the same way as with celery. It has a nutty taste and is usually served boiled. Up to eight trimmed sea kale stalks are tied together, then cooked in salted water for up to 20 minutes, or until it becomes soft. Sea kale can be served hot or cold, and goes well with salads or fish dishes.

Chapter Nine

BRADAN & CADAN

In Irish, the salmon is known as 'bradan'. Although this recipe is generally accepted as a Scandinavian dish, commonly known as Gravlax, named after the herb dill, the salmon of Ireland are ideally suited to marinating in the following way. It is also a tribute to the way that the Vikings finally settled down to live side by side with the Celts in Ireland, doing much to shape the country's culture, and embellishing its folklore with many Viking legends.

Dill (Anethum graveolens), grows to 18 inches, and has feathery leaves which are pungently aromatic and similar to anise in quality. An infusion of the leaves is said to soothe the stomach and stimulate the body's system. The light brown, aromatic seeds are also used in flavouring savouries, and assist digestion. Chopped dill leaves go well with fish dishes, and the herb is also used in the making of dill pickles and dill cucumbers.

Salmon trout, sea trout, and brown trout are commonly called 'breac geal' in Irish, and a variety of traditional salmon and trout dishes can be tasted at the Limerick Food Festival, held in June, or at the Kinsale International Gourmet Festival in October, or the Ballina Salmon Festival in County Mayo. Tarragon, (Artemisia dracunculus), is a strongly flavoured, perennial European herb, used sparingly in sauces and vegetable dishes. This bitter herb has overtones of liquorice and anise, and is used in the preparation of some sauces. Tarragon vinegar, a favourite fish accompaniment, can be made by steeping the herb's leaves in wine vinegar, while tarragon butter is also a traditional fish flavouring.

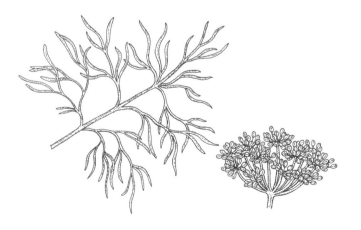

Right: the 'King of Fishes', the salmon, is known in Ireland as 'Bradon' and is simply prepared in a dish like Viking Salmon (see p. 118).

VIKING SALMON

A middle cut of fresh salmon, around 3 pounds
4 tablespoons of salt
1½ tablespoons of castor sugar
2 tablespoons of white peppercorns, crushed
3 tablespoons of fresh dill, chopped

Method: *Clean the salmon, slice in half lengthwise, and de-bone. Place one salmon piece, skin side down, in a casserole dish. Sprinkle the dill over the salmon flesh. Mix together the salt, sugar and peppercorns, then sprinkle the mixture over the dill. Place the second piece of salmon piece, flesh side down, on top of the first. Place a large plate on the top of the salmon sandwich. Place heavy weights on the plate to weigh the salmon down. Put the weighted dish in a refrigerator for 12 hours. Remove from the refrigerator, turn salmon over, and replace weighted plate. Replace in refrigerator for another 12 hours. Repeat this whole operation 3 more times over a 60-hour (2½-day) period. Once the fish is marinated, gently remove the salt and dill mixture by scraping it off the fish. Dry the salmon, then slice it very thinly. Serve with mustard sauce.*

The legendary warrior-king, Finn McCool, who acquired the salmon's knowledge, was the son of Murna, the daughter of a Druid who forbade her to marry. Murna eloped with her knight-lover, but he was murdered by the Druids, after which she gave birth to his son, whom she named Demna. Finnegas, a kind Druid, took in the mother and son, bringing up Demna as his own, and calling him Fionn, or Finn. On reaching adulthood, Finn joined a company of Celtic knights, known as the Fianna, or 'Fenians', at the court of the famous King, Cormac Mac Airt. Finn was elevated to the rank of Captain of the Royal Bodyguard after saving the King's life, and eventually went on to ascend the throne. Traditionally, Celtic kings were first 'married' to a white mare, the incarnation of Macha, the horse goddess, who taunted prospective lovers with demonstrations of her speed. After the 'wedding' the mare was ritually killed and eaten. However, Finn courted another goddess, Sadbo, who had been changed into a fawn by magicians. Sadbo changed back into a woman long enough to give birth to Finn's son, Ossian, or 'Little Fawn'.

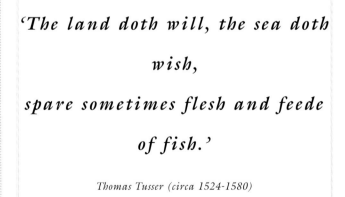

'The land doth will, the sea doth wish,

spare sometimes flesh and feede

of fish.'

Thomas Tusser (circa 1524-1580)

Right: Viking Salmon.

TARRAGON TROUT

2 fresh trout, cleaned
1 ounce of flaked blanched almonds
2 ounces of butter
½ lemon, cut in two
Juice of half a lemon
2 sprigs of fresh tarragon
4 sprigs of fresh parsley
1 small onion, sliced into thin rings
1 green bell pepper, cored, de-seeded and sliced
into thin rings
3 tablespoons of yoghurt
1 tablespoon of tarragon wine vinegar
1 hard-boiled egg, chopped fine
1 teaspoon of salt and freshly ground black
pepper, mixed

Method: *In each gutted trout cavity, place a tarragon sprig and a lemon quarter. Butter some cooking foil on a grill tray, place fish on foil. Put a little butter on each fish. Cook under a pre-heated grill for 5 minutes. Turn the fish and smear with more butter. Cook for another 5 minutes. Toss the almonds in a little melted butter and grill them until brown. Keeping the fish warm, heat the remaining butter in a small pan. Saute the onion and pepper rings, then mix in vinegar and yoghurt. Stir in the egg and seasoning, then heat gently. When sauce is hot, place fish on plates, and pour over the lemon juice. Place the sauce beside each fish, and decorate with the sprigs of parsley.*

Ireland's folklore is intermingled with tales of its various saints. Some of the stories are truly laced with legend, which is not surprising, considering that the Vikings, who eventually settled down with the Irish, devised their own saints, such as Saint Colmcille, and interwove their life histories with tales from the Norse legends. There is the story of Saint Kevin, a 6th-century hermit saint who apparently inhabited a cave in Glendalough, now known as Kevin's Bed. It is said that when he was disturbed from his 'bed', by a wandering pilgrim, he flew into a rage and hurled the unfortunate monk over a nearby cliff into Upper Lake. Another legend tells of the 5th-century Saint Buithe, one of Saint Patrick's followers, who was said to have ascended to heaven on a ladder, conveniently lowered down for him. It was Buithe whose name was believed to be the origin of the word Boyne, hence the name of the River Boyne. The nearby monastery was founded by St Buithe. In Galway, a bridge known as the Salmon Weir Bridge, was built in 1818 to link the jail with the courthouse and, upstream, is the famous salmon weir itself. The River Boyne is famous for its fine salmon and trout, and the following dish might be typical of the region.

An aromatic herb, Thyme (Thymus vulgaris), has a number of uses, and is used to flavour anything from chicken and veal, to vegetables, fish, and game. It is a particularly pungent herb and can be used, with other herbs, to make a bouquet garni. This ancient herb is also therapeutic, with antiseptic and antibiotic qualities. Bacterial, fungal, and viral infections can be treated both internally and externally with preparations made with this herb. Thyme is a digestive remedy for stomach cramps and diarrhoea, and is often used to treat colds and influenza.

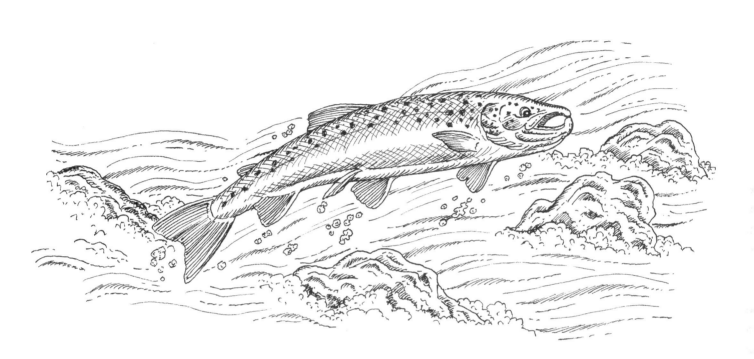

There is the tale of how the legendary Finn McCool acquired his celebrated knowledge. It relates how Fintan, the husband of the first invader of Ireland, Cesair, survived the biblical deluge by turning into a salmon. Transformed into the fish, he ate the 'Nuts of Knowledge', and thus became the 'Salmon of Knowledge'. The Druid, Finnegas, caught the fish in the River Boyne and gave it to Finn McCool to cook. Finn burned his finger whilst roasting the salmon. By sucking his finger, he gained the fish's wealth of knowledge and wisdom, becoming Fion, the 'Fair One'. This story may be heard at the Visitors' Centre at the Salmon Research Agency on Lough Furnace, County Mayo.

Fluthered, in local Dublin slang, means quite drunk, and the following recipe for marinating wild salmon includes a few generous nips of Irish whiskey. The sea salt in this recipe is sodium chloride, and is obtained from purifying sea water, then evaporating the water from the salt content. The salt is then graded into commercial and table salt. Table salt is available in coarse or fine grains. To make it easier to pour, the fine-grained salt is mixed with a little calcium phosphate and magnesium carbonate. These additives keep the salt dry, and stop it absorbing moisture and clogging together. This recipe, an Irish form of Gravlax, is made with coarse-grained sea salt, which is pure and contains no added chemicals.

FLUTHERED WILD SALMON

1 tail of wild salmon, around 3 pounds

5 tablespoons of coarse sea salt

3 tablespoons of Irish whiskey

2 tablespoons of soft brown sugar

1 tablespoon of lemon juice

2 tablespoons of freshly ground black pepper

2 tablespoons of fresh thyme, chopped fine

2 teaspoons of fresh dill, chopped fine

Method: *Scale, de-fin, and bone the fish, then divide it into two fillets. Mix together the salt, sugar, lemon juice and whiskey. Sprinkle the thyme and dill in the bottom of a large baking dish. Ladle 3 tablespoons of the whiskey mix over the thyme. Lay one salmon fillet on the thyme and whiskey mix, skin side down. Spoon more of the whiskey mix over the salmon flesh. Place the other fillet, flesh down, on the first fillet. Use the rest of the whiskey mix to coat the skin side of the top fillet. Place cooking foil over the dish, and place a heavy weight on the fish. Leave in a refrigerator or other cool place for the marinade to permeate the fish. After three days, remove fish, clean off marinade, and slice finely.*

Right:** some of the essential ingredients for* ***Fluthered Wild Salmon.

adan is the Irish word for herring and, from the Middle Ages until the late 1700s, Ireland exported vast numbers of salt fish, mostly sea fish, to the Continent. These fish were mainly herrings and cod from Munster and Connaught, and salmon, salted and exported from a large fishery in Galway. They were first gutted, then packed in barrels according to their size and quality. Today there are just two main fishing ports in the Irish Republic, and three in Northern Ireland. Although the island's waters are teeming with fish and crustaceans, fish recipes are few and far between. Until recently, the Irish have generally preferred meat and vegetable dishes to fish meals, as was the case even during the Great Potato Famine. However, the Irish have a long tradition of fishing and they still pickle or 'pot' herrings.

TIPSY CADAN

10 small herrings, cleaned
2 carrots, sliced
2 onions, chopped
1 onion, sliced
1 garlic clove, chopped fine
2 teaspoons of fresh parsley, chopped fine
1 pint of Irish stout
½ pint of light ale
1 teaspoon of dried thyme
1 bay leaf
4 black peppercorns
3 cloves
1 tablespoon of vinegar
1 teaspoon of salt and pepper, mixed

Method: *Mix carrots, chopped onions, garlic, herbs spice and seasoning in a pan. Pour in the stout, boil, then simmer until vegetables are cooked. Turn out into a large baking dish. Place the herrings on the vegetables, and cover with onion rings. Pour in the vinegar and the light ale. Bake in a moderately hot oven for 20 minutes. Let cool. Serve with soda bread.*

Mackerel or 'ronnach' in Irish, is an oily, round fish with a delicious flesh, preferably filletted before cooking. Most mackerel weigh around 1-1½ pounds and have distinctive steel-blue band across their backs, with a silvery underbelly. These fish are at their best between October and March, and provide a good source of protein. They also contain the vitamins A and D. Mackerel can be grilled, fried, baked or steamed, and the gooseberries and fennel in this following recipe are an ideal accompaniment.

Fennel (Foeniculum vulgare), is an ancient culinary and medicinal herb, and can be made into a tea, used in eye compresses, or as a fine remedy for wind and indigestion. The leaves sprout from a root, which, in one variety, Florence fennel (Foeniculum vulgare dulce), grows into a bulb, which is sweet, anise in flavour, and is eaten as a vegetable. Fennel's feathery leaves go well with any fish dishes. Fennel seeds, also used as a flavouring, can be chewed to aid digestion. As a traditional side dish, colcannon mash – the savoury Irish potato dish – makes an ideal accompaniment to the light, sharp, main course that follows.

RONNACH IN GOOSEBERRY SAUCE

2 fresh mackerel fillets, around 1 pound each
1 large onion, chopped fine
1 pound of trimmed gooseberries, halved
2 ounces of butter
2 tablespoons of breadcrumbs
2 tablespoons of sugar
2 tablespoons of water
1 teaspoon of grated lemon rind
1 teaspoon of fennel, finely chopped
1 teaspoon of salt and pepper, mixed

Method: *Cook the onion in the butter until soft. Add half of the trimmed gooseberries, season, and cook for 5 minutes. Stir in the breadcrumbs. Spread the paste on the flat mackerel fillets. Sprinkle fennel on the fillets, then roll them up. Place the rolled fillets on a baking dish, and bake in a moderate oven for 20 minutes. Stew the rest of the gooseberries with the sugar, water and lemon rind. After 10 minutes, or when the fruit is soft, liquidize in a blender. Serve the rolled fillets with the gooseberry sauce poured over them.*

The traditional west coast fishing vessel, which probably dates back many thousands of years, is known as the currach. The currach is a high-prowed fishing vessel, shaped like a large canoe, and is covered with tarred cloth. The making of currachs is a craft peculiar to the west coast of Ireland. These boats are wood framed and are still made to the original design in the sleepy little fishing village of Ballydavid, in County Kerry. In some places, the rounded, similarly-built coracle, like that made in Wales, is still in use, mainly for fishing on rivers or lakes.

Overleaf: the Irish have a long tradition of fishing.

Chapter Ten

CLASSIC SAUCES

It is recorded that, in 1780, a Reverend James Kenny, was building one of the first English-style herb gardens in Kilnanahee, were he grew pennyroyal, a form of mint, as well as balm, sage, thyme, rosemary, camomile and horehound, amongst other herbs. Around this time, there was a great interest in growing and documenting both traditional and unusual herbs and, throughout Ireland, most monasteries maintained extensive herb gardens. While Dublin, the 'city of pen and print', might have produced great literary luminaries like Swift, Moore, Goldsmith, Burke, Molyneaux, Shaw, Joyce, Yeats, Stephens, Wilde, Beckett, Gogarty et al, it also produced a plethora of herbalists and botanical artists. Many museums across Dublin celebrate the life and times of the country's greatest writers, and the oldest public library in the country, Marsh's Library, built in Dublin in 1701, and the Chester Beatty Library in the city, have fine collections of early botanical prints. Trinity College, Ireland's oldest university, founded by Queen Elizabeth I in 1592, also has numerous early volumes on botany and herbs amongst its 200,000 ancient books. For a selection of Irish literature and books on herbs, visit Hodges Figgis, Ireland's oldest bookshop, established in 1786 on Dawson Street, Dublin.

There are around seven types of mint, three of which are more commonly used in culinary concoctions. These are Spearmint (Mentha spicata), Peppermint (Mentha piperita), and Pennyroyal (Mentha pulegium). Spearmint aids digestion, and is used in a medicinal drink, and to stimulate the appetite. This mint is used in sauces and jellies to flavour meats, as are the leaves of the peppermint, which produces an important, mildly antiseptic essential oil. Peppermint tea, mint julep, and creme de menthe are among the numerous uses for this mint. The pungent pennyroyal variety was once used as a purgative for the blood. Mint sauces can be made in any number of ways, but the basic recipe combines the flavour of mint with vinegar and sugar, although some prefer it tart, without the sugar. The following mint sauce is classically used to accompany lamb and mutton.

Right: a ready supply of fresh herbs is essential for any student of Irish cookery.

Mint Sauce

2 tablespoons of fresh mint, chopped fine
2 teaspoons of castor sugar
4 tablespoons of vinegar
1 tablespoon of boiling water

Method: *Pound the mint with the sugar in a mortar. Set aside for 30 minutes. Add boiling water to dissolve sugar. Finally, stir in the vinegar.*

Oregano (Origanum vulgare), is really the common form of marjoram, and it grows wild in Ireland. It is the only form of this herb which is used medicinally, acting as a sedative. Oregano is a common ingredient in soups, sauces or gravies. This herb goes well with any meat, poultry, game, egg, or cheese dishes, but is not used in fish dishes or salads.

James Joyce (1882-1941), was one of the Dublin's leading writers, celebrating the city and people he knew in *Dubliners*, and the semi-autobiographical *Portrait of the Artist as a Young Man*. He was born at 41 Brighton Square, in the suburb of Rathgar, but left for Paris in 1902. Between 1903-4, Joyce returned to his Irish homeland briefly, beginning one of his earliest works, *Chamber Music*, in 1907. Seven years later, he penned the acclaimed *Dubliners*. *Ulysses*, written in 1922, was an intimate observation of 24 hours in the life of Dublin, as seen through the eyes of anti-hero, Leopold Bloom, celebrated by afficionados on 'Bloomsday', June 16th. However, when it was published, the novel received a bitter torrent of attack from both religious and literary pundits. Joyce once said that Dublin city could be rebuilt, should it ever be destroyed, by following the descriptions in *Ulysses*. His last book was *Finnegan's Wake*, a witty, yet convoluted tale which is arguably his most accomplished, yet least understood work.

Tartare sauce is a classic accompaniment for seafood, especially delicately flavoured fish like plaice. This sauce may be bought ready-made, but there is no substitute for the freshly made version, the recipe for which follows.

TARTARE SAUCE

2 eggs, hard boiled

1 raw egg yolk

1 teaspoon of capers, chopped

1 teaspoon of fresh parsley, chopped fine

1 teaspoon of chives, chopped fine

¼ pint of maize oil

1 tablespoon of vinegar

½ teaspoon of salt and freshly ground black pepper, mixed

Method: *Remove the yolks from the hard-boiled eggs, retaining one egg white. Rub the yolks through a sieve, then stir in the separated raw egg yolk. Stirring slowly, add the oil drop by drop until sauce becomes thick and smooth. Press one egg white through a sieve into sauce. Stir in the vinegar, then add parsley and chives. Add seasoning and capers.*

It was from the Americas that maize, like the potato and the tomato, arrived in Ireland to substitute the countryfolk's staple diet of potatoes. Before the Great Famine of the 19th century, the average household of six, including four children, would get through 252 pounds of potatoes a week, according to local records. Maize, or sweet corn, to give it its common name, was a brief substitute for the potato when the blight struck the country, and maize oil is now a common feature in local cookery and in the making of sauces.

Oscar Fingall O'Flahertie Wills Wilde (1854-1900), was born in Dublin and educated at Trinity College and Magdalen, Oxford. In Oxford he created the cult of 'Aestheticism', and became editor of *The Woman's World* in 1887. His tome *The Picture of Dorian Gray*, was published in 1891. After losing a libel case against Lord Queensbury, he was imprisoned in Reading Gaol in 1895, where he wrote *De Profundis*. On his release in 1897, he wrote the poem, *The Ballad of Reading Gaol*. He also wrote the plays, *Lady Windermere's Fan*, *A Woman of no Importance*, and *An Ideal Husband*. Wilde's play, *The Importance of Being Earnest*, published in 1899, was a tongue-in-cheek study of the British class system. Wilde died in the following year, 1900, while in exile in Paris.

On excavating the remains of part of 10th-century Dublin, remains were found which revealed that Ireland's Viking community not only enjoyed apples, but dined on strawberries, plums and cherries, as well as more exotic fruits, like grapes and figs. Sauce made from apples is a classic accompaniment to pork or goose and a traditional Irish recipe follows.

APPLE SAUCE

6 cooking apples, peeled, cored and sliced
1 ounce of butter
2 ounces of castor sugar
Rind of quarter of a lemon
4 cloves

Method: *Stew the apples, cloves, and lemon rind in a little water until the fruit turns to a pulp. Stir in the sugar, then press the sauce through a sieve, removing the cloves and lemon rind. Add butter and re-heat.*

Edmund Burke (1730-1797), the philosophic writer and orator, was born in Dublin and was educated at Trinity College. He left Ireland and became a member of Parliament in 1765, and made his name writing treatises, such as *A Vindication of Natural Society* and *Sublime and Beautiful*. Burke denounced the French Revolution in his work, *Reflections*. Thomas Moore (1779-1852), was born in Dublin, and also studied at Trinity College. He also moved to London, where he drafted a respected translation of *Anacreon*, and then to Bermuda. Moore then wrote a *Life of Byron*, and *Irish Melodies*, earning the accolade 'Bard of Erin'. It was Moore who wrote *The Vale of Avoca* and The *Last Rose of Summer*, legendary airs which have the typical lilting sound of early Irish music.

The Sunflower is a native of the Americas, as are so many common ingredients in Irish cookery, like maize or sweetcorn, the tomato and the potato. The oil which is pressed from the sunflower's tiny, highly nutritious seeds is widely used in cookery and sauces, and is light, with a faintly nutty flavour. Hulled sunflower seeds, which can be eaten raw, contain around 18% carbohydrate and 23% protein. The fully-grown sunflower is a very tall plant of the genus Helianthus. It blooms in a huge golden flower which has a large seed-bearing centre.

Horseradish is the hot, peppery and pungent root of a vegetable which is used in cookery, generally grated finely, and often used in vinegars, chutneys and pickles. Horseradish was traditionally raised in November, when the root would be steeped in vinegar for use during the winter months. The gratings are often mixed with cream to make a sauce. Horseradish contains vitamin C, and is a good diuretic, with antibiotic qualities. Care should be taken when preparing horseradish, as its vapour and juice can be very irritating to the skin, eyes, nose and throat. The following cold dish, either known as mould, or mold, takes the form of a complementary thick sauce, generally served as an accompaniment to roast dishes, especially roast beef, but it goes equally well with salmon.

HORSERADISH MOULD

2 tablespoons of freshly grated horseradish
3 tablespoons of double cream, whipped
3 ounces of gelatine
1 teaspoon of grated lemon rind
1 teaspoon of lemon juice
1 cup of boiling water
1 teaspoon of salt
4 drops of green food colouring (optional)

Method: *Dissolve the gelatine in the boiling water, then stir in the horseradish, lemon juice, grated rind and salt. Stir in the colouring. Pour into a mould and chill thoroughly before serving.*

Horseradish sauce is a traditional accompaniment to beef and cold meats, and is usually served cold. There are several recipes for horseradish sauces, some are made with herbs, some are served cold while others are meant to be served hot.

HORSERADISH SAUCE

3 tablespoons of freshly grated horseradish
1 teaspoon of mixed mustard
1 teaspoon of sugar
1 teaspoon of lemon juice
½ teaspoon of salt
½ pint of double cream, whipped
½ teaspoon of freshly ground black pepper
2 teaspoons of vinegar

Method: *In a bowl, thoroughly mix together all the ingredients except the whipped double cream. Gently fold in the cream, mixing it in well, then serve.*

Should the visitor to Ireland want to view a typical Irish merchant's kitchen of the 15th century, a faithful reconstruction can be seen in Dublina, an exhibition of the life and times of Dublin installed next to Christ Church Cathedral in Dublin. The Medieval Trust has accumulated a fascinating exhibition of the life and times of the city from 1170 to 1540. Georgian life in a fine town house can be experienced in Newman House in the city, as can domestic living between 1790 and 1820 at Number Twenty Nine, in Lower Fitzwilliam Street. George Bernard Shaw's Birthplace is a fine, authentic example of Victorian life and times, located in Synge Street, Dublin, where the house has been carefully restored to replicate the elegance of its era. Farther from the capital is the James Joyce Museum, located in the Napoleonic Martello tower, the setting for his first chapter of *Ulysses*. Also not far from Dublin, in the 1738 Ardgillan Castle, kitchens dating from Georgian and Victorian times can be viewed. In Newbridge house, built in 1737 just outside the capital, a reconstructed dairy of the period can be seen, with implements dating from early times. In 1690, near Dublin at Malahide Castle, 14 members of the Talbot family sat down to breakfast in the Medieval Great Hall. It was their last meal together, as every one of them was killed, later that very day, in the Battle of the Boyne.

> '*Make hunger thy sauce, as a medicine for health.*'
>
> Thomas Tusser (circa 1524-1580)

CLASSIC BROWN SAUCE

1 onion, chopped
1 carrot, sliced fine
2 rashers of bacon, chopped
1½ ounces of plain flour
1 teaspoon of tomato puree
1 pint of stock
2 ounces of dripping or butter
½ teaspoon of salt and freshly ground black pepper, mixed

Method: *Saute the onions, carrots and bacon in the dripping or butter until brown. Gradually stir in the flour and cook gently for 15 minutes, taking care not to let it burn. Slowly add the stock, stirring well until smooth. Add tomato puree, salt and pepper. Bring to the boil and simmer for 30 minutes. Strain the sauce through a sieve and serve hot or cold.*

HERRING ROE SAUCE

1 pint of Bechamel sauce
1 pound of soft herring roes
2 ounces of butter
1 tablespoon of mustard paste
1 teaspoon of lemon juice

Method: *Cook the roes in 1 ounce of butter over low heat. Press the roes through a sieve into the heated Bechamel sauce. Stir in the mustard and lemon juice. Melt 1 ounce of butter into sauce, stir in and serve.*

Right: Barbecued Irish mountain lamb is a perfect match for Classic Brown Sauce.

THE TOMATO STORY

The tomato (Lycopersicon esculentum) is a member of the Solanaceae family, which includes henbane, nightshade, chillis, peppers, aubergine, tobacco, and the potato. It is really the fruit of an herbaceous plant, native to South America, discovered by the Spanish during the conquest of Mexico, where it had been used for thousands of years. The tomato is now one of the most common food ingredients. When it was first brought to Europe in the 16th century, the tomato was named the 'pomme d'amour', or 'love apple', and was shunned by Cromwell's Parliament, which believed it to be morally corrupting, and spread false rumours that tomatoes were poisonous. The tomato will grow in most climates, and the fruit is generally green when unripe and red when ripe. However, there are numerous varieties of tomato, where colour varies, as does the shape. Most tomatoes are glossy-skinned and usually spherical in shape. The Currant and Cherry tomatoes are very small and round, compared to the Beef tomato, which can be twenty times the size of the Cherry. There are also the pear-shaped tomatoes, known as Plum, or Italian tomatoes.

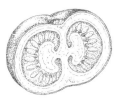

The leaves and stalk of the tomato contain poisonous alkaloids known as 'solanins', and it is only the fruit which is eaten. Tomatoes have a thin skin which can be peeled, a task made easier by blanching them in hot water. They also contain many edible seeds, which are indigestible. Tomatoes are rich in vitamins A and C, and iron, and are a source of sugar, with a high water content. Tomatoes are widely used in sauces, relishes, pickles, chutneys, and ketchup, or catsup. Fresh tomato sauce is traditionally served with veal or chicken, but can also accompany fish dishes.

TOMATO SAUCE

1 pound of ripe tomatoes, quartered

1 tablespoon of plain flour, mixed with 3 tablespoons of water

1 teaspoon of castor sugar

2 ounces of butter

1 rasher of bacon, chopped

1 onion, finely chopped

1 carrot, finely sliced

1 pint of chicken stock

½ teaspoon of salt and freshly ground black pepper, mixed

1 teaspoon of lemon juice

Method: *Fry bacon in half of the butter for 2 minutes, then add the onion and carrot. Saute for 5 minutes, add tomatoes, cover, and cook for 5 minutes. Stir in the stock, then stir in the flour mix. Add salt and pepper, lemon juice and sugar. Cover the pan and simmer for 30 minutes. Let the sauce cool, then press it through a sieve, discarding what remains in the sieve. Re-heat the sauce, then stir in remaining ounce of butter.*

Most of the following sauces are traditionally served with poached, baked, or steamed firm, white fish, with the exception of Tartare sauce, which is made in a different way, and is served cold. The choice of which fish or seafood is best served with which sauce, is a matter of personal taste. Traditionally, certain sauces are accepted as ideally suited to particular fish and seafood dishes. Many of these classic sauces are based on the White, or Bechamel sauce, a basic foundation for the following recipes. This sauce was said to have been invented in France, in the late 17th century, when Louis de Bechamel – Marquis de Nointel and a steward in the household of King Louis X1V – introduced it to the royal table for the first time. Bechamel sauce is easily made, and is used as the basis of more exotic sauces, like the delicate parsley sauce, used mainly for white fish.

Parsley Sauce

1 pint of Bechamel sauce
2 tablespoons of fresh parsley, chopped fine

Method: *Add the parsley to the Bechamel sauce and heat through gently.*

The Celts or Gaels of early Ireland, who named the River Shannon, were related to the Gauls of France and the Galatians, who received their Epistle from St Paul. However pagan the Celts might seem, it was they who established the first civilization north of the Alps. Their families, or 'derbfine', were grouped together in clans, or 'tuaths', overseen by a warrior king. It was the Celts who invented the first common market, initiated the first major industrial and agricultural revolutions with the introduction of iron, and began the first proper court. It was they who invented horseshoes, chain mail armour, and introduced soap to the inhabitants of the Mediterranean. The width of their iron-tyred chariots dictated the span of the first railways, and the inventions of the iron plough share, the wheeled corn harvester, and the rotary flour mill were also theirs. The Celts brewed ale and mead, developed the art of churning butter, and made unleavened bread. The Celtic judges' interpretation of the Brehon Laws provided compensation for any crime, even murder. The Celts also gave us the ancient sport of hurling, now the Irish national sport.

Bechamel Sauce

2 ounces of plain flour
2 ounces of butter, unsalted
1 small onion
4 cloves
6 peppercorns
1 pint of milk

Method: *Stud the onion with the cloves. Bring milk to boil with the cloved onion, peppercorns, and bay leaf. Remove from heat at boiling point, then let it stand for 10 minutes. Strain the liquid into a bowl. Heat the butter to foaming point in frying pan. Slowly stir in the flour to create a paste. Little by little, stir in the flavoured milk mixture, whisking constantly. Stir until the mixture is smooth. Pass mixture through a sieve to eliminate lumps.*

EGG SAUCE

1 pint of Bechamel sauce
3 eggs, hard boiled
1 teaspoon of salt and freshly ground black
pepper, mixed

Method: *Remove the yolks from the hard-boiled eggs. Heat the Bechamel sauce to below boiling, then reduce heat. Press the egg whites through a sieve into the sauce. Stir well, and increase heat to below boiling.*

Many Celtic sites still exist throughout Ireland, and not least of these are the island's 3,000 sacred wells. Before the arrival of Christianity, these wells were dedicated to the pagan Celtic gods, substituted by the names of saints around the 6th century AD. However, in the country, some local folk preserve the Celtic rite of circling the holy wells in a sunwise direction. It is still a tradition to seek healing from the well's water by leaving a coin, pin, or a token strip of cloth at the wellside. The hope is that when the rag disintegrates, the ailment will disappear with it. Some wells' waters are said to be endowed with qualities promoting fertility, while others have contraceptive attributes. One ballad tells of the quality of mastership in marriage when the water of a certain well is drunk after the wedding ceremony. One suitor is said to have arrived at the church for his wedding, only to find that his future wife already had a bottle of the special well water with her to ensure that she wore the trousers in the future household!

BÉCHAMEL & MUSTARD SAUCE

2 ounces of plain flour
2 ounces of butter, unsalted
1 small onion
4 cloves
6 peppercorns
1 pint of milk

Method: *Stud the onion with the cloves. Bring milk to boil with cloves, onion, peppercorns, and bay leaf. Remove from heat at boiling point, and let stand for 10 minutes. Strain the liquid into a bowl. Reduce butter to foaming in frying pan. Slowly stir in the flour to create a paste. Bit by bit, stir in the milk mixture, whisking constantly. Stir until the mixture is smooth. Pass mixture through a sieve to eliminate lumps. Continue recipe by using this as a basis.*

1 pint of Béchamel sauce made as above
1 teaspoon of mustard powder
1 small chilli pepper
2 egg yolks
6 ounces of double cream
3 teaspoons of malt vinegar
1 teaspoon of lemon juice

Method: *Make a paste with the mustard and vinegar. Mix the paste and lemon juice into the Béchamel sauce, then add the chilli. Bring to the boil and remove chilli. Reduce heat and stir in the egg yolks and cream. Heat sauce to just before boiling, then serve.*

ANCHOVY SAUCE

1 pint of Béchamel sauce
1 ounce of butter, unsalted
3 tablespoons of double cream
1 tablespoon of anchovy essence

Method: *Heat the sauce until just below boiling point. Melt the butter in the sauce. Add the cream and anchovy essence, stirring constantly. Simmer the sauce for around five minutes, without boiling.*

COCKTAIL SAUCES

The classic sauce for crab, prawns, peeled shrimp and lobster, is Cocktail Sauce. It is usually served with a sprig of parsley, with a slice or two of lime or lemon as a garnish – and to squeeze over the seafood. Here are two versions of the sauce, which could be served with Ireland's celebrated shellfish.

Sauce 1
2 tablespoon of double cream
½ pint of mayonnaise
1 tablespoon of tomato ketchup
1 teaspoon of Worcestershire sauce
1 teaspoon of Tabasco sauce
1 teaspoon of lime juice
1 teaspoon of salt and pepper, mixed
½ teaspoon of cayenne pepper
1 teaspoon of paprika
2 limes, quartered

Method: *Combine the first 8 ingredients together in a bowl. Beat until the mixture is smooth and evenly coloured. Spoon the mixture over prawns, shrimp, or lobster tails. Decorate with paprika and lime quarters.*

Sauce 2

3 tablespoons of mayonnaise

3 tablespoons of tomato ketchup

3 tablespoons of cream

1 teaspoon of Worcestershire sauce

1 teaspoon of lime or lemon juice

1 teaspoon of Tabasco sauce

1 teaspoon of paprika

Method: *Combine all ingredients together as a puree in a blender, or mix by hand, until the colour of the sauce is even. Use with seafood.*

Above: Cocktail Sauce is a perfect dressing for prawns.

Chapter Eleven

GAME & POULTRY

Ireland has long been an island of forests and mountains, ideal territory for natural game, like the pheasant, partridge, rabbit, hare, wild boar and deer, and these have attracted visitors over the centuries. Many tales have been told of the legendary qualities of Ireland's game. Large, fierce wild boars once terrorized the population, and it took two brave warriors to hunt and kill them. A Tuan MacCarell, when asked about his ancestry, told the tale of how he was once changed from a boar into an eagle, and then into a salmon, which was eaten by a woman who gave birth to him in human form.

An unfortunate culinary incident happened in Dunluce Castle, in Bushmills, Londonderry, in 1639. The lord's cooks were preparing a banquet in the kitchens, when that part of the castle collapsed, throwing all the kitchen workers off the cliff and into the sea far below. Soon after that, the turreted castle was abandoned and its gaunt ruins still show were the kitchen buildings once stood. In those days, although the potato had been in use in Ireland for little more than half a century, the aristocracy lived extremely well, with a multitude of local game to select from. Banquets in early times were lavish affairs, with salmon, trout, pheasant, partridge, quail, all manner of wild fowl, from duck to snipe, as well as rabbit, hare, and venison gracing the tables – unless of course, your kitchen disappeared into the sea before the meal reached the table!

In 1698, John Dunton, an English traveller in Ireland, recounts his experiences of staying with the Irish Offlaghertie (sic) family. He says that he was invited to walk a small mile to view their deer, and was surprised to hear of a Deer Park in such a wild place. However, after trekking through bogs and over mountains, the group arrives at Glinglass Vale, or the Green Valley, where they came across...

"...some hundreds of stately red deer, the stags bigger than a large English yearling calfe, with suitable antlers much bigger than I ever saw before."

Dunton says that it was the most pleasing scene that ever he met with in the kingdom, and after the group had retired for a vast dinner of beef and mutton, "myn host ordered his dogs to be gotten ready to hunt the stagg."

Right: Ireland has long been an island of forests and mountains, ideal territory for natural game.

FLUMMOXED VENISON

2 pounds of cleaned venison, hung for the pot
1 pint of mead, or red wine
1 pint of Irish stout
2 onions, chopped
2 carrots, chopped
4 tablespoons of plain flour
2 ounces of butter
1 ounce of cornflour
1 bouquet garni
1 teaspoon of salt and black pepper, mixed

Method: *Cut the venison into large cubes. Marinate in mead or red wine, bay leaves and bouquet garni overnight. After marinating, remove the meat, saving the marinade. Roll meat in the flour. In a frying pan, saute the meat in the butter, a few pieces at a time, until browned. Put the meat in a heavy pan. Pour the marinade over meat and add onions and carrots. Remove bouquet garni, then simmer meat until it is tender. Blend the stout with the cornflour, add to pan and bring to the boil. Season with salt and pepper, simmer for 2 minutes, then serve hot.*

Sage (Salvia officinalis) is a plant from Southern Europe with wide, bluish-green leaves, widely used in cookery. As it has a very pungent flavour, sage should be used sparingly. Its leaves can be dried and powdered, or used fresh. Sage preparations are also used as an antiseptic and anti-inflammatory in cases of sore throats and colds. The stout in the dish that follows gives it a typically Irish bite, and sage is the ideal complement to wild Irish rabbit.

Right: Flummoxed Venison is great served with new potatoes.

'We may live without poetry, music or art

We may live without conscience and live without heart

We may live without friends, we may live without books

But civilised man cannot live without cooks.'

'Lucille', The Earl of Lytton (1803-1873)

RABBIT PIE

4 ounces of ready-made puff pastry

4 portions of rabbit

2 ounces of butter

1 onion, chopped

2 ounces of bacon, chopped

6 ounces of mushrooms, sliced

2 tablespoons of cornflour

½ pint of chicken stock

½ pint of Irish stout

1 teaspoon of salt and freshly ground black pepper, mixed

A sprinkling of plain flour

1 egg, beaten

Method: *Fry the rabbit pieces in the butter until they are cooked and browned. Remove the rabbit, then fry the mushrooms, onion and bacon in the same butter. Put the rabbit, onion, mushrooms, and bacon in a pie dish. Mix the cornflour with the chicken stock. Pour this, and the stout, into the pie dish. On a surface sprinkled with plain flour, roll out the chilled puff pastry to fit over the pie dish as a lid. Dampen round the edge of the dish with water, then press the pastry down around the edges. Brush beaten egg over the pastry to glaze it. Make a hole in the centre of the pie to allow air to escape. Bake for around 25 minutes until the pastry is golden brown.*

There are fifty types of Basil, but two main varieties, Sweet Basil (Ocimum basilicum) and Bush Basil (Ocimum minimum), are the most commonly used. Basil is the traditional herb to use in tomato dishes, and it goes well with meat, egg, or cheese dishes. Basil is also used in a snuff concoction, to clear headaches, as an aid to digestion, and as a laxative.

A Basil vinegar is made by infusing leaves in wine vinegar for two weeks. Basil, a herb which goes very well with game, was said by Culpeper, the herbalist, to draw the poison from the bites of venomous beasts. This particular use is redundant in Ireland, where there are no snakes, let alone venomous ones, since St Patrick was alleged to have banished them from the land in the 4th century AD.

Oregano (Origanum onites), a branch of the marjoram family, is more usually known as Pot Marjoram, but it is Wild Marjoram which is more commonly called oregano. This herb is generally used with tomatoes and meat sauces, and can be used to flavour strong-tasting, closely textured fish. In the following dish, oregano complements the strong, gamey flavour of the hare.

May Day, or ancient Beltaine, was reserved as the only day for hare hunting and, even then, few people would eat the hares which they caught. This was because of a long-standing local superstition surrounding the magical qualities of the hare. In Irish folklore, a character named Caoilte once demonstrated his speed and agility by herding together all the rabbits and hares in Ireland. Today, most good game shops seem to have followed his example, and many butchers now specialise in game.

JUGGED WILD HARE

1 wild hare, jointed and cleaned

3 rashers of streaky bacon

1 pound of small onions, chopped roughly

1 clove of garlic, crushed with salt

½ pound of button mushrooms

2 ounces of butter

1 tablespoon of seasoned plain flour

1 ounce of margarine

6 peppercorns, crushed

1 teaspoon of dried basil and oregano mixed

1 bay leaf

3 tablespoons of stock

1½ pints of Irish stout

2 tablespoons of corn oil

Method: *Marinate the hare pieces overnight in stout, peppercorns, bay, basil and oregano, and oil. Fry the bacon in the butter for 3 minutes, then add the hare pieces. Brown the hare and remove from pan. Fry half the onions and garlic in the same fat. Return the hare to the pan, with the flour, then strain in the marinade. Bring to the boil and add stock. Cover and simmer for 3 hours. Add more stout if needed during cooking. Lightly fry the rest of onions and mushrooms in butter. Remove hare pieces when cooked, adding them to the onions and mushrooms. Heat marinade sauce until it is reduced and thick. Strain it over the hare and serve.*

Celtic priestesses often kept hares for divination purposes. They would secrete them in their clothing, often in the bodice, giving rise to the myth that hares were indeed the incarnation of the Devil, who would suckle at the women's breasts. Hares were also believed to drain the best calves' milk from milche cows. The priestesses would release the tamed hares and watch their movements as indications of prophecies. Later, many countryfolk believed that witches could turn themselves into hares, which is why some people would not eat hare.

Many of Ireland's legends and folk tales involve the island's prolific wildlife and game. Tales of the pursuit of young women by much older men are also prolific throughout Irish legends, especially in the one about *The Cycle of Finn, Ossian, and their Companions.* In part of this tale, The Pursuit of Diarmuid and Grainne, Finn McCool, together with his son, Ossian, and grandson, Oscar, are all warrior heroes. Finn, however, is elderly, although betrothed to a young local beauty named Grainne. In those times, wild boar hunting was a common pursuit in Ireland, but Finn had other quarry in mind. Grainne had eloped with a young warrior from his own band, Diarmuid. At first, the youngster was loath to run away with his lord's betrothed, but Grainne enticed him with a 'geis', or spell. For 16 years, Finn McCool pursued the couple, and each time he drew near to capturing the lovers, Diarmuid would kiss Grainne, sending Finn into a fury.

At last, Finn seems resigned to the fact that Diarmuid would remain with Grainne, and suggests that the young man joins him in a wild boar hunt. A magnificent boar had been sighted, but nobody had been able to track it down, until Finn and Diarmuid come across its track. As the two men approach the boar, Diarmuid realises that he has left his favourite spear at home. The boar turns on the youngster, and mortally gores him with its tusks. Diarmuid knew that Finn had special powers which could save his life – if Finn would only bring him a drink of water with his own hands. Finn refused, Diarmuid died, and Finn finally married Grainne as he had promised many years before.

Above: a wild Boar hunt, from a 17th century painting by Frans Snyders.

Wild boars once represented fertility, courage and wealth and are found represented in Celtic statuary, particularly those commemorating celebrated warriors. Ancient Druids used the right shoulder blades of black boars for divinations known as 'slinneireachad.' In County Sligo there is a place called the Black Pig's grave, possibly named after a Celtic boar hunt that ended there. The bristle of the boar was once given magical qualities and the mythical hero, Fion, died by stepping on a boar's bristle or 'friuch', after breaking a 'geasa' or local law against hunting boars. When the legendary Princess Isolde dreamed of a great boar hunt, her dream was interpreted as a forewarning of the death of her lover, Tristan, who was a mighty boar hunter, formerly banished by her father the King.

Although the wild boar has been extinct in Britain and Ireland for many centuries, cuts can now be obtained in specialist shops. However, wild boar was prevalent in the country when the English Normans invaded Ireland, and their traditional Christmas dish was stuffed wild boar's head, served with laurel and rosemary sprigs. This popular culinary herb (*Rosmarinus officinalis*) has numerous culinary uses, and is particularly good with lamb and roast pork dishes. Rosemary is said to improve the memory, and an oil derived from rosemary is made into a tonic for digestive, nervous, and circulatory problems. The oil is also used to treat hair loss, wind, headaches and arthritis. Wild boar was a favourite with the legendary Irish warrior kings, as in the story of Finn McCool. Boar has a dark, lean meat, stronger than pork, with a rich, gamey flavour.

GRILLED WILD BOAR STEAKS

4 steaks of wild boar, around 8 ounces each

4 springs of rosemary

6 juniper berries, chopped finely

1 teaspoon of paprika

2 tablespoons of vegetable oil

1 tablespoon of clear honey

1 tablespoon of Irish whiskey

1 teaspoon of salt and pepper, mixed

Method: *Mix together the oil, juniper berries, honey, whiskey, paprika, salt and pepper. Clean the boar steaks, drain and dry. Brush the steaks on both sides with the mixture. Place one steak on a large piece of foil. Pile the rest of the steaks on top of each other. Pour any excess marinade over steaks. Wrap the foil around the steaks. Leave to marinate in a refrigerator for around 3 hours, then remove the steaks and place them on an oiled grill over hot coals. Pour over any excess marinade. Cook for about 6 minutes each side. Serve garnished with the rosemary sprigs.*

In one Celtic legend, the two mythical pig farmers, Friuch and Rucht, both bitter rivals, were named after the bristle and grunt of the boar. It was said that they could change themselves into a variety of animals, including a boar, in order to disguise themselves when they battled for supremacy. It is said that a boar's bristle was reincarnated as Donn Cuilnge, who was sent to defeat Rucht. The story of Donn Cuilnge is often linked with Deirdre's tale, just one of the legends in the three Circles of Irish myths which involve pretty young maidens and ageing warriors. After the saga of the brown bull, or Donn of Cooley, Ulster's King Conchobhar, now in his dotage, went in search of a new wife. He quickly set his sights on Deirdre, a legendary Irish girl, said to be the most beautiful in the land. However, her beauty was marred by the fact that she was destined by a curse, or 'geis', to wreak evil. When promised to the elderly King Conchobhar, she was willingly abducted for seven years by the young King Naoise, who was killed by an act of treachery. Deirdre killed herself before she was forced to marry the older king.

Lovage probably arrived in Ireland when the Romans occupied England, as it was one of their favourite herbs. It has a warm, aromatic flavour and the stems, seeds and leaves of this tall plant are all used. Lovage (Levisticum officinale) is good in soups, stews, casseroles and salads. Treatments for the circulation and the kidneys are made from Lovage, which was the flavouring in an ancient cordial, once popular as a digestive. Lovage tea can be savoury, served with salt and pepper, or sweet, with honey or sugar. The leaves, which resemble coriander, and the stalk can both be used as a vegetable. Lovage imparts a full, meaty flavour to sauces and gravies, and a lovage soup can be made from the leaves by boiling them in water and adding cream.

'It is not how long you live, but how well you live.'

John Ray (1628-1705)

PARTRIDGE POT

2 partridges, prepared for cooking
4 ounces of streaky bacon
½ pound of shallots, peeled, with 2 chopped fine
½ pound of button mushrooms, washed, and
with stalks separated
1 ounce of butter
1 pint of stock
1 tablespoon of plain flour
1 tablespoon of lovage, chopped fine
1 teaspoon of salt and black pepper, mixed
Juice of half a lemon

Method: *Dice half the bacon, then heat it in a in a casserole dish. Add the partridges and brown all over. Add all of the unchopped shallots, and the mushroom caps. Pour in half the stock and add the lovage. Cover the dish and cook in a slow oven for 2 hours. Heat the rest of the bacon with the butter and 2 chopped shallots. When shallots are brown, add the mushroom stalks and the rest of the stock. Bring to the boil, stir in flour, then simmer until thick. Stir in some of the liquid from the partridge, and the lemon juice. Season the sauce and strain it over the partridges before serving.*

The tradition of the ancient Irish bards and poets, continued until the late 18th century, through a time of increasing political unrest. It was through their poets that the Irish could voice their many grievances against the English. Ireland's poets invented a form of rhyme or tale which disguised the true meaning of the story of oppression by veiling the plight of Ireland in legends, folklore and mythology, in the 'aislings', or vision-poems. All aislings took the same form: the poet relates how he falls asleep, waking in one of Ireland's sacred sites, where he meets a beautiful woman who is the personification of Ireland. The woman tells the poet how she was forced to marry a wicked dullard. However, there is a brave prince living across the sea (the Stuart King), who is avowed to rescue her from her plight. This tale is told in a multitude of ways, in which the inventive poets weave a story laced with prophecies, charms, spells, and romance. One of the most celebrated aisling poets was Egan O'Rahilly, who lived from about 1675 to 1729.

The two varieties of Savory (Satureia hortensis and Satureia montana) are both natives of Southern Europe. The leaves of this herb are used in many bean recipes, and are good with meat, poultry and game dishes as they have a faintly spicy, peppery flavour. The volatile oil in savoury aids digestion, and can be used to relive the pain of insect stings. In the following recipe, savory is used, along with other herbs, in a bouquet garni to bring out the gamey flavour of pheasant.

POT ROAST PHEASANT

1 large pheasant, dressed for the pot
2 eating apples, peeled, cored and quartered
1 onion, chopped
4 teaspoons of plain flour
1 tablespoon of butter
1 tablespoon of brown sugar
2 tablespoons of vegetable oil
1 pint of red wine
Juice of an orange
½ pint of stock
1 teaspoon of salt and freshly ground black
pepper, mixed
1 bay leaf and 1 sprig each of thyme, savory,
and parsley, tied to make a bouquet garni

Method: *Brown the pheasant in a pan in the hot oil and butter. Place pheasant in a casserole with the apple quarters. Saute the onion in the butter and oil. Slowly stir in the flour, then the stock. Add the wine, then the sugar and orange juice. Season with salt and pepper, and pour over the pheasant. Add the bouquet garni. Cover the casserole with its lid and cook the pheasant in a medium oven for 1 hour. When pricked on the leg, the flow of clear juices should tell that it is done. Remove from casserole, discard herbs, and serve.*

Named after the legendary Queen Macha, Armagh is Ireland's religious centre, selected by St Patrick in AD445 as the country's ecclesiastical capital and seat of learning. Ireland's second most important religious site is Clonmacnois, in County Offlay, founded by St Kieran, in AD545. Located on the banks of the River Shannon, this is the burial place of the ancient Kings of Connaught and Tara, and was chosen by St Kieran after he had a vision of a great tree growing in the middle of Ireland. Centred around a small cathedral, the site is dotted with mausoleums, temples and graves, including that of

St Kieran, who died just seven months after founding Clonmacnois. Three memorial crosses around the cathedral date from the 9th and 10th centuries, with one thought to have been erected by King Flann, who died in AD916. One of the crosses is decorated with a figure thought to be the Celtic god Cernunnos, who also appears on the Cross of St Adamnan, in the ancient citadel of Tara, which was also the burial ground of kings.

The third, or South Cross, is similarly decorated to the elaborate South Cross at Kells, and both are thought to date from the 9th century. Across Ireland, the fine art of ancient Celtic stonemasons can be seen on lonely crosses standing like sentinels in the windswept countryside. Two of the most impressive of Ireland's thousands of stone crosses are the two at Monasterboice, just north of Dublin, overlooking the Boyne Valley. With scenes depicting biblical events, one of the crosses date from the early 10th century, while the other, with 50 carved panels, is one of the tallest of the high stone crosses of Ireland, standing more than 25 feet high.

In north Connemara, County Galway, the ruins of a castle with a fascinating history stand on an island in Lough Corrib. This is Hen's Castle, defended by Grace O'Malley against the Welsh Joyce clan in 1570, and later against an English assault. After the Joyces had murdered Grace's husband, the English set siege to Hen's Castle. Grace had the castle's lead roof melted down, then poured it, red-hot, onto the enemy's forces. Meanwhile, a man was sent through a long underground tunnel to the shore, there to light a beacon summoning help.

In some parts of Ireland, the details of finance and the dowry, discussed before the wedding, is known as 'plucking the gander', and there is a legendary tale told at many a wedding breakfast. It relates that a couple were returning from their wedding when they spied a goose in a puddle.

"Do you see those two geese?" the wife asked her husband. Although he told her that the second goose was only a reflection, the wife insisted that there were two geese. At home, she was taken fatally ill, and on her deathbed she swore that there had been two geese. Just before the lid was put on her coffin, her final words, whispered to her husband, were, "There were two geese." Even as the husband walked beside his wife's coffin on the way to the grave, he thought he heard his wife insist that there were two geese. The morning after the burial, the husband returned to his wife's graveside. Clearing the earth from the coffin, he opened the lid and asked, "Are you still alive, wife?" "There were two geese," came the faint answer. The couple went home together and the subject of the geese was never mentioned again.

Because a cooked goose produces so much fat, many people shun this bird. However, the fat produced by any webbed-footed bird, like duck or goose, is not the harmful kind found in meats. A 'green goose', is one killed before it is 3 months old, and a 'gosling' is less than 6 months old. The best goose is that which is no more than a year old, with yellow feet. As a lot of fat is exuded from a roasting goose, the amount of meat is comparatively quite small, and an 8-pound goose is needed to produce enough meat for four people. The goose fat should regularly be removed from the roasting pan whilst cooking.

GAELIC ROAST GOOSE

1 oven-ready goose, around 8 pounds
1 ounce of butter
1 lemon, cut in quarters
1 pint of stock
1 glass of port
1 teaspoon of salt
1 teaspoon of freshly ground black pepper
1 teaspoon of ground ginger

For the stuffing:
2 onions, chopped fine, and boiled
1 pound of potatoes, boiled and mashed
1 pound of sausage meat
4 ounces of double cream
2 teaspoons of dried sage
1 teaspoon of salt and black pepper, mixed

Method: *Mix the stuffing ingredients together, and fill the goose with it. Truss the bird tightly, sewing each end. Mix the ounce of butter with the pepper, salt and ginger. Spread this mix over the bird's breast, then place it in a roasting tin. Add the stock to the dish. In a pre-heated oven, cook in a moderate heat for 2 hours. Pour the fat from the tin, then pour over the port. Cook the goose for another half hour until skin is crisp, then serve hot.*

The warriors of Celtic mythology devised various methods of capturing game birds. It was said that the chieftain, Cu Chulainn, was surpassed in his skill at catching wildfowl by his son, Connla. Connla could not only hit a flying bird with a stone, he could also stun them with his voice. Some Celtic heroes also learned how to interpret birds' songs, and could thus be warned of approaching danger by the changes in a bird's notes. Birds were also blamed for bad harvests, as in the case of the failure of Ulster's crops in ancient times, when, it is said, nine scores of birds consumed the land's fertility. In another myth, Deirdre dreams of three great birds which arrived bearing gifts of honey, and left taking blood. This was interpreted to reveal the treachery of King Conechobar.

HONEY TRUSSED CHICKEN

1 oven-ready chicken, medium sized
3 tablespoons of olive oil
2 tablespoons of clear honey
2 tablespoons of fresh basil, parsley and marjoram, mixed
1 lemon, halved
4 bay leaves, broken
2 sprigs of fresh rosemary
1 teaspoon of salt and freshly ground black pepper, mixed
1 teaspoon of sea salt

Method: *Rub sea salt inside the chicken's large cavity, then place one half of the lemon inside the cavity. Then insert the rosemary sprigs and bay leaves. Lastly, place the other half of the lemon inside the chicken. Carefully tear back the skin from the top of the chicken breast. Mix the olive oil with the honey. Sprinkle the salt and pepper mix on each side of the exposed breast. Drizzle half the honey and oil mix over the exposed breast. Sprinkle in half the herb mix, then replace the skin over the breast. Slash the thighs three times each side. Rub the rest of the herb mix into the cuts. Rub the remaining honey and oil mix over the chicken skin. Place the chicken, breast upwards, in a baking dish. Cook in a pre-heated hot oven for 5 minutes. Turn the chicken breast down, and cook for 5 more minutes. Turn chicken breast up, and cook for 1 hour, or until the skin is golden brown and the juices run clear.*

WILD DUCK WITH BABY TURNIPS

A medium-sized wild duck, trussed and
prepared
4 slices of bacon
3 carrots, sliced
2 onions, sliced in rounds
2 glasses of cider
1 stick of celery, chopped
2 glasses of brown stock
24 whole baby turnips

Method: *Arrange the bacon, celery, carrots, onions and bay leaf in a casserole dish. Place the duck on this and cook on the stove for 10 minutes. Pour the cider over the duck and cook to reduce the juices. Then pour the brown stock over the duck, put on the casserole lid, then cook it very gently for 1 hour. Meanwhile, cook the turnips in boiling salted water for 10 minutes. When the duck is cooked, take it out of the casserole and set it aside. Put the vegetables and liquid through a sieve to make a sauce. Skim off any fat. Place the duck back in the dish with the sauce, then add the turnips. Cook until the duck is very hot and serve immediately.*

Overleaf: Honey Trussed Chicken.

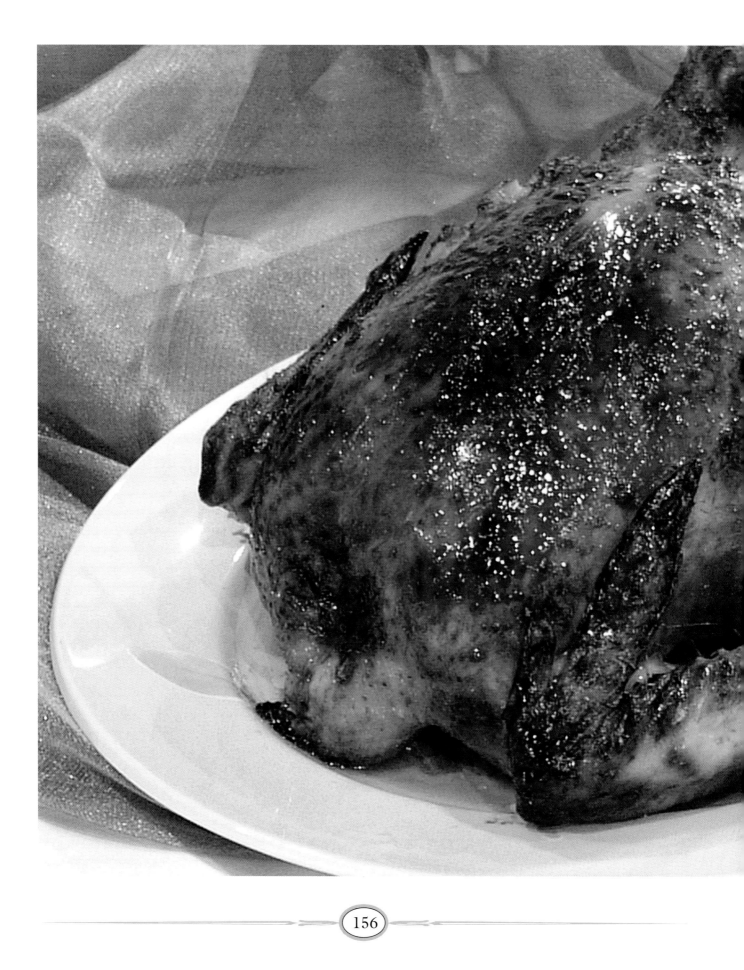

Chapter Twelve

DESSERTS & DRINKS

Natural beauty thrives under Ireland's 'soft weather', a colloquialism for 'damp climate', and there are few pleasures more enjoyable than a visit in a two-wheeled, horse-drawn 'jaunting car', to Torc Waterfall, in County Kerry. Ireland is rich in natural wonders, and its magical landscape has long been celebrated by numerous artists and enthused over by a multitude of poets, bards, and writers. The island's temperate climate is warmed by the North Atlantic Drift, and its rainfall swells famous rivers, like the Liffey and the River Shannon.

One of the most impressive natural sights in the country is that of the spectacular 700-foot high Cliffs of Moher, facing the legendary Aran Islands, in County Clare. Towering peaks can be climbed in the famous Mountains of Morne, which 'lead down to the sea', or in the beautiful Wicklow Mountains. At Downpatrick Head, in County Mayo, the Polnashantinny is a subterranean cave leading out into the Atlantic Ocean, from which pours clouds of spume as the sea rushes in. There are more ancient caves at Kesh, where the King of Ireland, Cormac MacAirt, was said to have been raised by she-wolves. Another famous cave system is the Desmond and New Cave complex, in which tunnels and caverns are covered in stalactites and stalagmites. In the Connemara region, there are the Twelve Pins, or Twelve Bens, quartzite peaks which boast the Banbaun, a central spire that rises 2,395 feet.

Two of Ireland's most scenic routes include a tour of the Nine Glens of Antrim, and a 100-mile circuit around the Ring of Kerry on the Iveragh Peninsula. From the heights of the Macgillycuddy Reeks, to the Lakes of Killarney, known as 'Heaven's Reflex', Ireland's soft air breezes through a land of spectacular scenery.

Right: Ireland's spectacular natural phenomena include the Giant's Causeway, which, in mythology, was created by Finn McCool. There is also the Giant's Throne, the Giant's boot, and even the Giant's Mouth Organ.

'*Did you treat your Mary-Ann*

To dulse and yelloe man

At the ould Lammas Fair in

Ballycastle?'

Early Irish children's rhyme

YELLOW MAN

1 pound of golden syrup
1 pound of brown sugar
1 large tablespoon of butter, melted
1 teaspoon of baking powder
2 tablespoons of white vinegar
2 drops of rose essence

Method: *Coat the inside of a pan with the melted butter. Pour in the syrup, sugar, rose essence, and then the vinegar. Bring to the boil and reduce to simmer. With a wooden spoon, drop a little of the mix into cold water. If it sets in the water, add the baking powder, stirring. When the mixture foams, pour it into a greased dish. When cool, pull the toffee-like mix until it turns yellow. Let it set, then break it into small pieces with a hammer.*

Rose essence would be often be added to the recipe for Yellow Man, or 'Yaller Man', a centuries-old confection, long associated with Ballycastle's 'Ould Lammas Fair', in County Antrim. The Lammas Fair, founded by special charter in 1606, is a mixture of a two-day cattle fair and a celebration of Irish music, dance and drink! Food fairs across the country offer the visitor a slice of Irish country life, and a chance to sample the local fare, like that at the two September Oyster Festivals, one in Clarinbridge, and the other in Galway. This county also holds the Hooker Regatta in June, a fine occasion to partake of traditional Irish cookery, or there is Kinsale's International Gourmet Festival, held in October, where a mixture of classic Irish dishes, and the country's 'nouvelle' cuisine can be sampled. At the August Puck Fair in Killorglin, on the Iveragh Peninsula, a billy goat is the centre of attention as it is sat on a chair throughout the festivities, as if on a throne.

Rose oil is an essential oil made from the petals of the rose (Rosa damascena and Rosa centifolia). Sometimes used in confectionery cookery, it can also be used as a cooling and calming agent on the skin. Infusions of rose petals are used in cosmetics as an astringent, and in medicinal preparations for soothing. The hedgerows of Ireland are often dotted with the boughs of the wild dog rose, from which some countryfolk still gather the hips, or haws. Rose hips, or the fruit, are high in vitamin C content, and rose hip syrup is used medicinally, and in ice creams and puddings. The rose hip has a thin red skin and a delicate pink flesh, which should be carefully separated from the pips inside, which are covered in irritant furry, or hairy filaments. When making oil or rose hip syrup, the hairs must be carefully separated from the flesh and skin, which are the only parts used.

George Bernard Shaw (1856-1950), was born in Dublin, and moved to join his mother in London at the age of 20. He first began a career as a novelist, although his first five novels were not published for many years. Shaw later embarked on a political phase, joining the Fabian Society. After writing essays on Ibsen and Wagner, he started out as a playwright in 1892. Shaw's first success was with *The Devil's Sorcerer*, which opened in New York in 1897. His most famous works are *Man and Superman* (1903), *Major Barbara* (1905) and Pygmalion (1916), on which the 1964 film *My Fair Lady* was based. One of his masterpieces was banned in Britain until 1925, as *Mrs. Warren's Profession* was centred around the oldest of professions, prostitution. One of Shaw's last works, penned in 1930, was *The Apple Cart*.

On food, that other great Dubliner, Jonathan Swift, once proclaimed, "Promises and pie-crust are made to be broken."

IRISH APPLE CAKE

2 cooking apples, peeled, cored and chopped

1 egg

4 ounces of butter

4 ounces of sugar

2 tablespoons of soft brown sugar

8 ounces of plain flour

1 teaspoon of baking powder

3 tablespoons of milk

3 cloves

Method: *Mix the flour and baking powder, then rub in the butter. Add the white sugar to the flour mix. Stir in the egg and enough of the milk to make a dough. Grease a pie dish and roll out half the dough to line it. Put the apples in the lined dish, sprinkle them with brown sugar and add cloves. Roll out remaining dough and cover the pie, sealing the edges with a little milk. Cook for 40 minutes in a in a hot oven until browned.*

Right: Irish Apple Cake.

There are several locations in Ireland where the visitor can witness first-hand the true taste of old Ireland and its culture. The Irish National Heritage Park, at Ferrycarrig, provides an illuminating insight into Irish life in its early settlements, reconstructing life from Viking times to the Middle Ages. At the Folk Village in Glencolumbcille, there are a number of reconstructed thatched cottages, furnished in period style from the 1720s, 1820s and 1920s, showing how Irish folk lived over the centuries. The Ulster History Park traces human history in Ireland from 8,000BC to the 1600s.

There is also the Kerry Bog Village at Glenbeigh, an authentic display of Irish home life in the early 19th century. There is the Bunratty Folk Park, where cottages depict life in the early 19th century, as well as the Touraneena Heritage Park. Other examples include the Lismore Castle Heritage Centre and Kenmare's Heritage Centre. Irish culture can also be experienced at the Bru Boru Heritage Centre, and Celtic dance, mime and music can be witnessed at the National Folklore Theatre in Tralee. For a true taste of Irish desserts, there is the Malahide Food and Drink Affair, held in Dublin, or the Strawberry Fair in County Wexford.

'Coleridge holds that a man cannot have a pure mind who refuses apple dumplings. I am not certain but he is right.'

'Essay of Elia', Charles Lamb (1775-1834)

IRISH COFFEE MERINGUE

3 egg whites

3 ounces of castor sugar

3 ounces of icing sugar

1 tablespoon of instant coffee powder

½ pint of Irish double cream

2 tablespoons of Irish whiskey

Method: *Whisk egg whites until stiff, then fold in the castor sugar. In another bowl, sift the icing sugar and mix with the coffee powder. Mix the icing sugar and coffee with the egg mixture. Spread the mixture in two separate round mounds on baking foil. Cook both in a very low oven for 4 hours. When the two rounds are hard and dry on the outside, but soft inside, remove from oven and set them aside. Whip the cream until stiff, then mix the whiskey into it. Spread the cream on the flat side of one meringue round. Form a sandwich by placing the second meringue on top.*

During the 1200s, the waters of the Poddle River, in Dublin, provided the raw material for ale brewing, which was fast becoming the national drink. By the mid-1660s, Dublin was the centre of the Irish ale business and there were more than 90 brewpubs in the city, plus almost 2,000 ale houses, in a city of just 4,000 families. During the mid-18th century in London, an ale made popular by the fruit and vegetable porters of Covent Garden, and those working in the fish market at Billingsgate, became known as 'porter'. The addition of roasted barley to the ale gave the drink a distinctively dark colour and a slightly malted, or toasted, taste. Back in Dublin, a man named Giles Mee was brewing an ordinary ale on a site near the city's old entrance, St James's Gate, as early as 1670. The brewing rights were transferred to Sir Mark Rainsford in around 1693, and the business remained in the family until the brewery was leased to a John Paul Espinasse, in 1715. On his death, in 1750, the brewery went into disuse for ten long years. In country parts of Ireland, the following recipe with stout is traditionally held to prevent colds.

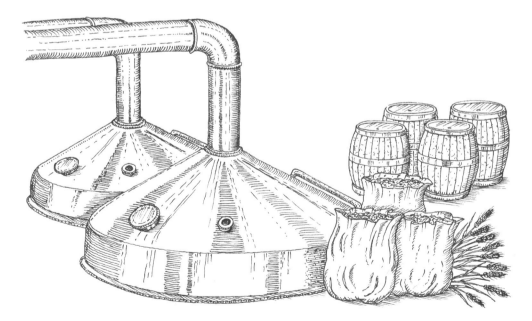

STOUT BERRY

2 tablespoons of rolled oats
2 tablespoons of brown sugar
1 teaspoon of fresh root ginger, chopped fine
1 teaspoon of freshly grated nutmeg
Juice of half a lemon
2 pints of stout

Method: *Heat the stout in a pan and stir in the oats, ginger and nutmeg. Boil, then simmer for 20 minutes. Strain the stout into a warm jug, then stir in the sugar, honey and lemon juice. Serve while still very hot.*

'...Till the live-long daylight fail,

Then to the Spicy, Nut-brown ale.'

John Milton (1608-1674)

In Dublin, in 1759, a 34-year-old Irishman named Arthur Guinness decided that the English were not the only ones able to brew a fine porter, and approached the owner of the derelict St James's Brewery. With true Irish optimism, Guinness signed a 9,000-year lease on the brewery, agreeing to a rent of £45 a year. To see this lease out, Arthur Guinness would have to live until he was 9034 years of age, beating Methuselah by 8065 years! However, he began his business by first brewing a traditional Dublin ale, and later developing a strong porter which he named 'extra stout porter', later shortened to 'stout' or 'Guinness stout'. The popularity of his new brew overtook that of the local ale, and was soon being transported around Ireland through the newly constructed network of canals. At the ripe old age of 78, Arthur Guinness passed away in 1803, handing the business over to his son, also named Arthur. At the time of Arthur Guinness's death, his favourite porter, or stout, was enjoying a brisk export trade, with Guinness West Indies Porter being shipped under sail to the thirsty folk of the Caribbean.

CRANACHAN

4 tablespoons of whiskey
4 tablespoons of honey
2 ounces of almonds, toasted and chopped fine
3 ounces of rolled oats, toasted
12 ounces of double cream
1 teaspoon of lemon juice
1 slice of orange

Method: *Whip the cream stiffly in a bowl, then fold in honey and whiskey. Stir in the rolled oats and the almonds, then the lemon juice. Serve chilled, garnished with the orange slice.*

The Guinness strong Foreign Extra Stout (FES), with a 7.5% alcohol content, is brewed in much the same way as the 18th-century porter. FES was developed by Arthur Guinness II, especially for the export trade. The stout is matured for three months in wooden barrels, and then blended with a young stout. In the early part of the 19th century, Beamish and Crawford of Cork, was brewing 100,000 barrels of stout a year, while the Guinness factory was producing 66,000. But by 1833, the Guinness brewery had become the largest in Ireland and, just after Arthur Guinness II died in 1855, during the latter half of the 19th century, it was the largest brewery in the world. The Guinness brewery, re-vamped in 1886, even contained its own railway! So popular was the Guinness stout in England that a branch of the brewery was opened in Park Royal, London, in 1936. Guinness went on to establish more breweries abroad, including those in Nigeria, Malaysia, Cameroon, Jamaica and Ghana. Guinness is now brewed in more than 45 countries and in all five continents, and you can buy Guinness in any one of 55 different countries.

Guinness stout contains all-Irish products: 90,000 tons of home-raised barley are used each year, as are the local hops and yeast, and Ireland's famous water. The Brewery stands near the banks of Dublin's River Liffey, although the water used in brewing comes from the Wicklow Mountains. Guinness begins as a sweet liquid known as 'wort', made by straining a 'mash' made from roasted and milled barley and water, through a device known as a 'kieve'. Hops are added to the wort, before it is boiled in huge kettles, or coppers, for an hour and a half. The wort is then settled for around 40 minutes and left to cool. Yeast is then used in the fermentation process, converting the nutrients and sugars in the wort into alcohol and beer – literally turning wort to best!

An unfermented wort, known as 'gyle', is then added to the beer, which undergoes a second fermentation, and matures. The beer is now clarified and, most importantly, tasted, before distribution. Whilst Guinness is the beer of 'Dublin's Fair City', Cork has the two major breweries, Beamish and Murphy's, and there are several breweries in Ulster. Two of the more renowned are the Herald brewery at Lisburn, and Hilden's brewery in Coleraine.

As its name implies, the following recipe for Stout Ciste contains lots of stout. 'Ciste' is the name for cake in Irish, this one eaten as a dessert at the end of a meal. It is best served with a generous dollop of fresh Irish cream.

Right: Irish Guinness enjoys both a brisk export trade and remains a local favourite to many of its countrymen.

STOUT CISTE

1 pound of plain flour
8 ounces of butter
8 ounces of brown sugar
8 ounces of raisins
8 ounces of sultanas
8 ounces of currants
2 ounces of glace cherries, quartered
1 teaspoon of allspice
1 teaspoon of bicarbonate of soda
3 eggs, beaten
1 bottle of stout, 12 ounces

Method: *Put the stout, sugar and butter together in a pan on a low heat. Stir until butter melts, then mix in the fruit and bring to boil. Simmer for 4 minutes then let mixture cool. Line a greased medium baking tin with greaseproof paper. Mix the flour, allspice and bicarbonate of soda in a bowl, then add the fruit mixture. Stir in the eggs, mixing well, then turn mixture into the baking tin. Bake in a medium oven for 2 hours, testing with a knife. Leave to cool, then turn out and slice to serve.*

Apart from Guinness, there are several other well-known stouts made in Ireland, including that of Lane's Southgate Brewery, in Cork, established in 1758. This business was taken over by Beamish and Crawford, which was initially the Cork Porter Brewery, founded in 1792. The country's second largest brewers, James J Murphy, was established at Lady's Well, in Cork, in 1856. Murphy's began by brewing porter, but switched to stout as its popularity grew. Another newcomer to the Irish stout scene is Caffrey's, and there are several other independent breweries, like Smithwicks, Hilden of Coleraine, Herald at Lisburn, and Whitewater, which brew ales, stout, and porter. One definitely un-Irish drink, popular almost everywhere, is Black Velvet. Made with equal quantities of iced stout and champagne, traditionally the stout and champagne should be poured into the glass simultaneously, and not stirred, but drunk whilst the bubbles remain, and before the drink goes flat.

'Yet may this cup of whey,

O Lord serve as my ale-feast

Fathoming its bitterness,

I'll learn that you know best.'

Attributed to the Hag of Beare

All the by-products of brewing go back to the land. Farmers use, as animal feed, the 'screenings' – barley too small for brewing, the 'combings' – little roots grown by the partially germinated barley, the waste produced after yeast is added to the wort, known as 'trub', as well as the surplus yeast. Therefore, in the process of brewing stout, nothing is wasted. The final product itself, the celebrated Irish stout, is the ideal accompaniment to Ireland's traditional fare, especially cheese, meat dishes, and seafood, which is why stout is often called 'The Essence of Good Living'.

Irish whiskey, spelled with an 'e', as opposed to the Scotch 'whisky', was the favourite whisky of the English. As far back as the 16th century, Queen Elizabeth I once announced that Irish whiskey was her only true Irish friend. Irish whiskey has been distilled from a base of barley and malted barley in Ireland for centuries, and whiskey records date back as far as the the 6th century.

Barley was known to be cultivated in Ireland as long ago as 3,000BC. Ireland's contribution to the world's alcoholic tapestry is its fine whiskey. It is not known exactly when the first distiller produced Ireland's famous spirit, but it certainly pre-dates the days of those individuals whose life was centred around spirits of a different kind, the Druids. In the 1st century AD, the Greek scholar, Diocorides, noted that the Irish were drinking a brew of malted barley, flavoured with herbs, known as 'curmi'. Later on, in the 4th century, Saint Patrick himself was said to have employed a brewer, when he returned to spread Christianity in Ireland.

Unusually, Irish whiskey is made with a barley which does not have the smoky, peaty content of whisky. This is because the grain is dried on a solid floor over fires, which prevents the smoke from permeating the barley. Irish whiskey differs from the Scotch variety, in that it is more industrial, and employs indirect coke heat to dry the grain, whereas the Scots are the more agricultural producers, drying grain over peat fires. This is the opposite of what one would expect, as peat is so naturally associated with Ireland, which cuts more than 5 million tons of peat per year, mostly for electricity production. However, the Irish method ensures a smoothness which the Scots' peat fire heat cannot attain. Also, most Irish whiskey is pot stilled three times, and matures for around five years before reaching the market. The oldest whiskey distillery in the world is Bushmills, located in Belfast, on the banks of the River Bush. The company was licensed to distil whiskey in 1608. Ireland's special spirit was popular in England up until the very early 20th century, when a Royal Commission sat to discuss the subject! The Commission, headed by the London Borough of Islington, permitted the raw, batch-distilled malts of Scotland to be blended with lighter whiskies produced from other grains.

The following recipe for Hot Irish, known in olden times as 'scailtin', would ideally finish off a meal of crubeens, or pig's trotters, especially at a family celebration. In the early days, this concoction might have been served at the many local 'shebeens' or small taverns which sold whiskey illicitly. It would be supped from a 'madder' or 'mether', a wooden drinking cup, the name of which comes from 'meadar', the vessel from which mead was originally drunk.

Hot Irish

1 extra large measure of Irish whiskey
1 teaspoon of demerara sugar
6 cloves
1 teaspoon of freshly grated nutmeg and
cinnamon, mixed
1 slice of lemon

Method: *Warm a sturdy glass with very hot water. Then fill it two-thirds with boiling water. Dissolve the sugar in the water, then add the whiskey. Add the lemon slice, nutmeg and cinnamon, stirring gently. Hold in the hand, savour the aroma, sip slowly. Now order another!*

Note: This classic preventative for the common cold is best enjoyed at a typical 'craic', or Irish gathering of local dance, song, and convivial conversation, all in the presence of a 'seanachai', or travelling storyteller, the modern equivalent of the ancient bards, or filis. As Saint Augustine once said...

"Give me chastity and continency – but not yet!"

Right: Drawing off malt samples at a distillery.

TIPSY PUDDING

For the Pudding:
3 ounces of flour
3 ounces of castor sugar
2 tablespoons of cornflour
3 eggs
1 pound of fruit jam
1 teaspoon of corn oil
1 teaspoon of vanilla essence
4 fluid ounces of Irish whiskey
3 fluid ounces of sherry

For the Topping:
1 tablespoon of sugar
1 teaspoon of cornflour
10 fluid ounces of milk
2 egg yolks
10 fluid ounces of double cream
2 ounces of blanched, roasted almonds
½ teaspoon of vanilla essence

Method for pudding: *Line a wide, flat baking tin with corn-oiled cooking foil. Pre-heat the oven to hot. Whisk sugar and eggs together thoroughly, in a bowl over hot water. Fold in the flour and vanilla essence. Pour the batter into baking tin. Bake for about 8 minutes until done. Turn out onto a cornflour-dusted surface. Remove the foil. Spread jam over surface of cake, and roll cake into a Swiss-roll. Set on a dish to cool, then pour whiskey and sherry over the top.*

Method for topping: *Whisk the eggs, cornflour, sugar and vanilla essence together. Beat in the milk and set the bowl over a pan of simmering water. Stir until the mixture is thick. Pour the mixture over the roll and refrigerate it for 1 hour. When chilled, spread cream over pudding. Decorate with roasted almonds.*

There are three main distillers of whiskey in Ireland, of which the best known are Dublin's Powers, and Cork's favourite Bushmills and Jameson labels, with numerous ages and types of whiskey coming from County Antrim. There is also the Paddy range of whiskies, as well as Redbreast, Green Spot, and Tullamore Dew. Those not so well known include Connemara, a single malt which has a local, peaty flavour, similar to the blended Irish Inishowen. The Derry single malt, made by the same distillers, and known as Tyrconnell, has an oily, or woody flavour, and they also produce an excellent light whiskey, named after an old Dublin tipple, Millar's. Then there is the Kilbeggan, with a delightful aroma, all produced by a 10-year-old distillery on the Cooley peninsula, near Dundalk, County Louth, in the east of Ireland. The Cooley whiskies are aged in the original Locke's Distillery in Kilbeggan, County Westmeath.

The first chocolate drinking house opened in London in 1657, and it was not long before Dublin had its own Chocolate Houses. Chocolate was a popular but expensive drink for a century or so, until tea and coffee became fashionable.

'On firm land only exercise your skill,

There you may play and safely drink your fill.'

Epitaph to a drowned, drunken fiddler

WHISKEY CHOCOLATE CAKE

1 pound of dark, unsweetened chocolate
1 pound of digestive biscuits, crushed
2 eggs
2 ounces of butter
6 tablespoons of castor sugar
8 fluid ounces of whiskey
3 tablespoons of double cream
4 ounces of whole hazelnuts
2 ounces of crushed hazelnuts
2 ounces of glace cherries

Method: *Whisk the eggs and sugar together. Melt the butter and chocolate in a pan, and fold in the egg mix. Mix in the crushed hazelnuts and fold in half the whiskey. Line a greased cake baking dish with crushed biscuits. Pour the chocolate mixture into the dish. Place in refrigerator overnight. Mix the remaining whiskey with the cream. Remove cake from refrigerator and pipe top with the cream. Decorate with whole hazelnuts and cherries, and serve.*

The eminent poet, Alexander Pope, was a particular friend of Jonathan Swift, whom he met in 1712, the year before Swift was ordained as Dean of Dublin's Saint Patrick's University. The two became lifelong companions, after their first meeting when Pope was producing his famous work, *The Rape of the Lock.* They probably spent hours in the capital's numerous coffee shops, discussing theories which they had encountered on their travels. In 1726, Swift's masterpiece, *Gulliver's Travels* was first published. In the early days of the trans-Atlantic clipper flights, it is said that Irish coffee was served first to airline passengers landing at Shannon Airport, Foynes, from America. There are now a number of ways of making the perfect Irish Coffee, or Gaelic Coffee. The following is just one recipe.

"A little learning is a dang'rous thing;
Drink deep, or taste not the Pierian spring;
There shallow draughts intoxicate the brain,
And drinking largely sobers us again."

"Coffee, (which makes the politician wise,
And see thro' all things with his half-shut eyes)."

Alexander Pope (1688-1744)

IRISH COFFEE

2 tablespoons of Irish whiskey
2 teaspoons of brown sugar
Fresh, strong coffee
Fresh double cream

Method: *Warm a coffee cup or stemmed glass with hot water. Pour in the whiskey, then add sugar. Pour in the coffee, leaving a space two fingers wide at the top. Top up with cream poured over the back of a teaspoon.*

> ### 'There's more friendship in a glass of whiskey than in a barrel of buttermilk.'
>
> *Old Irish saying*

Hospitality goes hand in hand with the Irish, who have innumerable forms of greeting. Many salutations have a religious context, like 'May God speed you', 'God and the Blessed Virgin attend you', or 'Safe home to you by the help of God'. Ireland's patron saint is sometimes included, as in 'The blessed Patrick go with you'. Drinking each other's toast is a common Irish custom and in the early days, the peasant's raised drinking vessel would have been a wooden mug, or madder.

However, in the grand country houses, some drinking glasses were long and thin, without a base, and the drinker would have to sup the entire contents before replacing it on the table. More than a few toasts with this form of drinking glass would be unwise! As in every country in the world, the Irish have their form of 'Cheers', and a toast is drunk with the word 'Slainte!' meaning 'good health!'

'Here's brandy! Come, fill up your tumbler,

Or ale, if your liking be humbler,

And, while you've a shilling,

Keep filling and swilling,

A fig for the growls of the grumbler!'

From the drinking song by John O'Toumy (1708-1775)

'O, Toumy! you boast yourself handy

At selling good ale and bright brandy,

But the fact is your liquor

Makes every one sicker,

I tell you that, I, your friend Andy!'

*From Andrew MacGrath's reply to O'Toumy's drinking song. O'Toumy was landlord of a popular inn,
a meeting place for poets during the 1700s. His tavern was located in Mungret Street, Limerick,
and many a bard learned his art at O'Toumy's bar.*

Most people have heard of the clandestine distilling of an alcoholic spirit in Ireland, known as 'poteen', or 'poitin', which means 'little pot still'. This came about many years ago, when the tax on whiskey became unacceptably high. With possibly more names than the number of confirmed accounts of encounters with 'little people', 'holy water' and 'mountain dew' are just two terms for poteen, that classic Irish distillation. Poteen is pronounced 'potcheen', and is made to a number of local recipes, of which there are several combinations. Thought to date from the 6th century, when grain was the main ingredient, most poteen recipes include potatoes. This home-brewed spirit has been illegal in Ireland since 1661, under King Charles II's laws. But today, a form of commercially made poteen can now be purchased.

In one of these recipes, the 'usquebagh' or 'uisce beatha', or 'water of life' begins its life as a 'wash' of grapes, raisins, treacle, sugar and yeast in water, which ferments for three weeks. Forty gallons of this mash will produce a dozen bottles of undiluted poteen. The wash is strained into a boiler, when it is heated to boiling and begins to give off steam. The steam is then channelled into a long, spiral, copper pipe, known as the 'worm', which runs down into a barrel filled with cold water. When the hot steam cools suddenly, it condenses inside the tube, and can be tapped off as a clear, 140+ degrees proof, poteen. As the poteen begins to flow, the first couple of pints are too powerful to drink!

However, after this has been bled off, the tipple becomes weaker and more palatable. The 'run', as it is called, takes around three hours from boiling to bottling. The poteen is then tested for strength and taste. It alcoholic purity is first tested by dipping a twist of paper in the brew, then lighting the twist. The blue flame should not consume the paper. Secondly, a finger is subjected to the same treatment, and the tester should remain unscathed by the ordeal. The third – and best – test is to sample the poteen by drinking it!

Poteen should definitely not be used for the following recipe, and I have yet to find a traditional Irish food recipe which calls for poteen. Surely this is testament that it remains the favoured drink of traditional Ireland!

IRISH WHISKEY SAUCE

1 teaspoon of cornflour, mixed in a tablespoon
of orange juice
2 ounces of butter
2 tablespoons of orange juice
2 ounces of icing sugar, sifted
2 tablespoons of Irish whiskey

Method: *Melt the butter in a pan and add the orange juice, sugar and whiskey. Heat, stirring, until the sugar melts, then stir in the cornflour mix. Cook, stirring, for 2 minutes until sauce thickens, then serve.*

One of the earliest cereals to be cultivated, oats have been used as fodder for both man and beast for many millennia. Oats contain valuable vitamin B, calcium, carbohydrates, iron, fat and protein. Generally oats are ground into a flour known as oatmeal, or the grains can be passed through heated rollers to make rolled oats. Oatmeal is made by grinding the hulled grains, and it comes in a variety of forms. There are the fine, medium and coarse grades, and all are used to make breads, porridge, broths, scones, cakes, and all manner of bakes. The Gaelic Atholl, or Atholl Brose, is claimed by the Scots, but brose is originally thought to have come from Ireland. Oatmeal, cream, honey and Irish whiskey are the main ingredients of brose, although there are many variations. The oatmeal is steeped in boiling water, then strained, and the cream, honey and whiskey added to the pulpy results.

Brose has traditionally been held to be a remedy for the common cold, and its name may have derived from the word 'Ambrosia' or 'Food of the Gods'. Other experts suggest that the name brose stems from the word broth, and, in Ireland, to be called a 'broth of a fellow', is a compliment, as it means you are a really fine fellow.

IRISH BROSE

2 tablespoons of Irish whiskey
1 tablespoon of runny honey
3 tablespoons of rolled oats
10 ounces of double Irish cream

Method: *Leave the oats in boiling water for 1 hour, then pour them into a sieve. Press down with the back of a spoon until most of the water is expelled. Whip the cream and fold in the honey and whiskey. Stir in the oats and serve.*

COOKERY NOTES

The recipes in this book are derived from numerous sources. While some are from friends and acquaintances whose traditional recipes have been handed down through their families, others have been researched to be as authentic as possible. Just as the Irish language varies throughout the island, and in those countries which have large Irish populations, so the recipes vary from place to place in their ingredients, proportions of measures, and methods of preparation. Unless indicated otherwise, the recipes in this book are either for four people, or are part of a main dish.

COOKERY ALTERNATIVES & FOOD SUBSTITUTES

The following British and American terms and words are more or less interchangeable.

EQUIPMENT AND TERMS

BRITISH	AMERICAN	BRITISH	AMERICAN
baking tray	cookie sheet	liquidize	blend
cake tin	cake pan	mince	grind
cling film	saran wrap	minced	ground
cocktail stick	wooden toothpick	mould	mold
cooking foil	aluminium foil	muslin	cheesecloth
dressed weight	ready-to-cook	packet	package
flan tin	pie tin	piping bag	pastry bag
frying pan	skillet	polythene	plastic
greaseproof paper	waxed paper	pudding basin	pudding mold
grill	broil	top and tail	stem and head
kitchen paper	paper towels	whisk	whip or beat

INGREDIENTS

Alternative ingredients are indicated in brackets.

BRITISH	AMERICAN
Aubergine	eggplant
Bacon rasher	bacon slice
bannock	round, flat cake
bicarbonate of soda	baking soda
biscuit	cookie
black olives	ripe olives
boar steak	(pork steak, beef steak)
broad beans	(fava, lima or java beans)
Cake mixture	cake batter
castor sugar	(granulated sugar)
celery stick	celery stalk
chicory	endive
chilli	chili pepper
cod, codling	(hake, haddock)
cornflour	cornstarch
courgettes	zucchini
Demerara sugar	brown sugar
double cream	heavy whipping cream
dripping	meat drippings
Essence	extract
Farls	quarters
fat	shortening
flounder	(mullet, plaice, snapper, sole)
Gelatine	gelatin
gherkin	sour pickle
golden syrup	(light corn syrup)
green grapes	white grapes

INGREDIENTS

BRITISH	AMERICAN
Haddock	(cod, hake)
ham	smoked ham
hard-boiled eggs	hard-cooked eggs
haricot beans	(navy, or white beans)
herring	(mackerel)
Icing	frosting
icing sugar	confectioner's sugar
Jam	preserves
joint	roast of meat
Kippers	kippered herrings
Lard	shortening
ling	(cod)
Mackerel	(herring)
mashed potatoes	creamed potatoes
minced beef	ground beef
mince	ground beef
mixed spice	allspice
monkfish	(dogfish, skate)
Peeled prawns	shelled shrimp
plaice	(flounder, snapper, sole)
plain flour	all-purpose flour
Rasher of bacon	slice of bacon
root ginger	ginger root
Salt beef	corned beef brisket
self-raising flour	all-purpose flour with baking powder
shortcrust pastry	basic pie dough
single cream	light cream
soft brown sugar	light brown sugar
spring onion	scallion

INGREDIENTS

BRITISH	AMERICAN
stewing steak	braising beef
stock cube	bouillon cube
stoned	pitted
streaky bacon	(regular bacon)
sultanas	seedless white raisins, golden raisins
swede	rutabaga
sweetcorn	corn, maize
Tomato puree	tomato paste
treacle	molasses
Unsalted butter	sweet butter
Vanilla pod	vanilla bean
Wholemeal	wholewheat

A VISITOR'S GAELIC GLOSSARY

It is always useful, not to say courteous, to learn a few words of the native language when visiting a foreign country. The following are a few of the more commonly used Gaelic words and their translation, which may help the visitor to become more immersed in the authentic feel of Ireland. Some words also indicate the original meanings of place names, giving an insight into the relationship of the land to settlements. Pronunciation may vary from place to place, therefore local advice should be sought.

GAELIC	APPROXIMATE ENGLISH TRANSLATION
Aelm	elm tree
Aer Lingus	Irish national airline
aglish	small church
ardhigh	point of landscape
ath (atha)	river crossing
Bainin	undyed wool
bairm breac (barm brack)	speckled cake
balriver	mouth
ballina	river ford
bally	Anglicised version of baile, or village
beg	small
beith	beech tree
ben	mountain peak
blarney	gift of 'silver tongue'
bodran (bodhran)	small, hand-held drum
Bord Failte	Irish Tourist Board
boreen	country lane
bun	end of road, river, or foot of a hill
Cairn	pile of stones as a marker or grave
carr	horse-drawn cart
carrig (carrick)	rock
Cead mile failte!	Ten thousand welcomes
ceidhle	traditional music and dance
cill (kill)	small church
clachan	hamlet
clogh	stone
clon	meadow
cnoc (knock)	hill
coiblide	Irish champ
coll	hazel tree
craic (crack)	animated friendly conversation
culchies	countryfolk
currach	small boat of canvas-covered frame
curragh	low, flat land
Dainsear!	Danger!
dankey	slightly drunk

GAELIC	APPROXIMATE ENGLISH TRANSLATION
derg	red
derry	oak tree
dolmen	prehistoric grave of large stones
drum	small hillock
drumlin	round, hilly mound
du (dub, duf, duv)	black
dun	fort
Eire	Republic of Ireland
Eirann	Irish
ennis (innis, inis, inch)	island
Failte	welcome
feis	gathering
feis ceoil	musical gathering
fiddle	violin
filidh	story-teller, bard
Fir	(Men) as in toilets
fleadh	musical festival
flummoxed	bewildered
fluthered	drunken state
Gaeltacht	old Irish language
gallan	pillar stone
Garda	Police
Geill Sli	Give Way (roadsign)
geis	curse
glasghaibhlinn	good pasture grass
glen	valley
High Cross (English)	tall stone cross
hurling	national sport like hockey
Keel	narrow
kelp	seaweed
ken	head (knowledge)
kets	variety of breads

GAELIC	APPROXIMATE ENGLISH TRANSLATION
Leprechauns	little people, fairies
lieter (letter)	hillside
lough (loch)	lake
Lughnasa	local word for harvest festival
Mac	son of
madder	wooden drinking vessel
miodh	mead
mona	peat bog
monastir	monastery
mor	large
Mna	(Women) as in toilets
Oifig an Phoist	Post Office
oughter	upper
owen	river
Pattern	Saint's Day festival
peat	brown earth of ancient rotted vegetation
poteen	distilled potato spirit
Quern	small stone grinding mill
Roe (rua)	red
ross	promentory, or copse
Round Tower (English)	early cylindrical stone tower
Scaithog	wicker basket
seanachai	travelling story-tellers
shane (shan)	old
shebeen	small tavern
side car (jaunting car)	pony and trap (carriage)
skerry (skerrig)	crag
Slainte!	Cheers! Good health!
slane	peat-digging spade
sliotar	hurling ball
slugane (sloke)	seaweed
spoileensmall	joint of meat

GAELIC	APPROXIMATE ENGLISH TRANSLATION
sproal	joint of meat
strand	beach, shore
Teampull	church
tra	shoreline, strand
tull (tully)	little hill
troander	whey
turf	peat
tweed	strong woollen fabric
Uilleann pipes	elbow pipes, like bagpipes
uisce beatha	water of life, whiskey
Victualler	butcher's shop

OTHER USEFUL EXPRESSIONS

balls of malt	whiskey
dead on	just right
dip	bread fried in a pan
feed	meal
fog feed	extravagant meal
half sir	landlord's son
jar	a couple of drinks
lashins	plenty
paralytic	drunk
tipsy	rather drunk

INDEX